THE WORST-CASE SCENARIO
ALMANAC
GREAT OUTDOORS

The
WORST-CASE SCENARIO
ALMANAC
GREAT OUTDOORS

By David Borgenicht
& Trey Popp

Illustrations by Brenda Brown

CHRONICLE BOOKS

SAN FRANCISCO

Worst-Case Scenario® and The Worst-Case Scenario Survival Handbook™ are trademarks of Quirk Productions, Inc.

Library of Congress Cataloging-in-Publication Data available.
ISBN-10: 0-8118-5827-8
ISBN-13: 978-0-8118-5827-4

Manufactured in Canada
Typeset in Adobe Caslon, Bundesbahn Pi, Futura, and Zapf Dingbats
Designed by Karen Onorato
Illustrations by Brenda Brown
Graphs illustrated by Bob O'Mara

Visit www.worstcasescenarios.com

Distributed in Canada by Raincoast Books
9050 Shaughnessy Street
Vancouver, British Columbia V6P 6E5

10 9 8 7 6 5 4 3 2 1

Chronicle Books LLC
680 Second Street
San Francisco, California 94107
www.chroniclebooks.com

WARNING

When a life is imperiled or a dire situation is at hand, safe alternatives may not exist. To deal with the worst-case scenarios presented in this book, we highly recommend—insist, actually—that the best course of action is to consult a professionally trained expert. But because highly trained professionals may not always be available when the safety or sanity of individuals is at risk, we have asked experts on various subjects to describe the techniques they might employ in these emergency situations. THE PUBLISHER, AUTHORS, AND EXPERTS DISCLAIM ANY LIABILITY from any injury that may result from the use, proper or improper, of the information contained in this book. All the answers in this book come from experts in the situation at hand, but we do not guarantee that the information contained herein is complete, safe, or accurate, nor should it be considered a substitute for your good judgment or common sense. Nothing in this book should be construed or interpreted to infringe on the rights of other persons or to violate criminal statutes; we urge you to obey all laws and respect Mother Nature.

—The Authors

CONTENTS

ფ "Men wanted for hazardous journey. Low wages, C8
bitter cold, long hours of complete darkness. Safe return
doubtful. Honour and recognition in event of success."
ფ C68

—Ernest Shackleton, advertisement for crew
for 1914 Antarctic expedition

INTRODUCTION

Most of us think of the great outdoors as a place we can escape to—a respite from the so-called real world. We go outdoors for solitude, for exercise, to commune with nature—to see stars and wildflowers, to breathe clean air, to take a walk in the woods. But the reality of the great outdoors can be somewhat different. From time to time, as history reveals, the great outdoors is a place you need to escape *from*. As Kurt Vonnegut once wrote, "If people think nature is their friend, then they sure don't need an enemy."

And it's not just wild animals that are the problem. It's also the weather. The rough terrain. The heat *and* the humidity. The rockslides and avalanches and floods. It's even the manhole covers and the pigeons in the city. It is a dangerous world outside your front door, no matter what environment you're setting off into.

But it's even more dangerous if you don't know what you're headed for. And that's where this book comes in. The only way you'll be truly prepared to leave the safety of your domicile and set a course, intentionally or unintentionally, for adventure is to learn everything you can about what you might encounter out there. Using this handy almanac, you'll be armed with the skills and information you need to make it back alive from the mountains, the arctic, the forest, the tropics, the desert, the ocean, and the urban and suburban jungles. You'll learn how to run rivers, survive lightning storms, build shelters, fend off animals, even keep beverages cool in the desert.

The Worst-Case Scenario Almanac: Great Outdoors also gives you additional equipment for your journey—the facts, statistics, charts, diagrams, and inspiring true tales of survival that will provide you with the information and stamina to avoid the pitfalls that befell those who came before you.

You'll be amazed at the stories within that demonstrate the power of the human will to survive: hiker James Scott, who survived for forty days without food when lost in a Himalayan blizzard; Aron Ralston, who amputated his own arm to escape from under a boulder; and seven fishermen who survived when their boat was capsized by a whale.

You'll be shocked to discover that many common survival tips are based on *myth* rather than *fact*. We've also provided you with fascinating insights into the worst nature has to offer—the most dangerous places, the most venomous snakes of the tropics, the times and temperatures that cause frostbite, the depths of the deepest ocean chasms. Our hope is that you'll be better able to embrace the planet's beauty and still emerge intact (or at least alive) to head for home.

Although this almanac is chock-full of information and survival advice, it is portable enough to fit into your rucksack, your harness, or your kayak. Like nature itself, it is exciting, instructive, and delightful—but our book is much safer.

And in a pinch, it can always be used as kindling—or toilet paper.

—The Authors

CLIFFHANGER

WORST AVALANCHES IN HISTORY

Location	Year	Casualties
Swiss Alps	218 BC	18,000 soldiers in Hannibal's army, about 2,000 horses and elephants
Disentis, Switzerland	1459	16 people, the 665-year-old Church of St. Placidus
Splügen Pass, French Alps	1800	56 soldiers in Napoleon Bonaparte's army
Wellington, Washington	1910	96 people, several train cars
Italian/Austrian Alps	1916	10,000 soldiers
Blons, Austria	1954	200 people, 90 houses
Ranrahirca, Peru	1962	4,000 people, the entire village
Yungay, Peru	1970	20,000 people, the entire city

MYTH: A loud noise can trigger an avalanche.

FACT: The common belief that loud noises can trigger avalanches is not supported by science. Under specific conditions, a sonic boom may have the potential to set off a snow slide, but unless a high-performance fighter jet breaks the sound barrier directly over a high-risk area, you needn't worry.

CLIMBERS ENDURE NINE AVALANCHES ON ALASKAN PEAK

On April 14, 1989, David Nyman and Jim Sweeney set out in Alaska's Denali National Park to climb the north face of a challenging peak known as Mount Johnson. As Sweeney was climbing a chute called the Elevator Shaft, the 35-foot-tall sheet of ice he was scaling collapsed, dropping him 100 feet down. His anchor rope stopped his fall, but the ball of his femur wrenched out of his hip socket and Sweeney was knocked unconscious. Lacking a radio, Nyman pulled his partner to safety, revived him, and skied down the mountain in a futile bid for help. Sweeney stayed behind, unable to walk. The next morning Nyman returned, placed his friend in a nylon sling, and began dragging the injured man toward civilization as snow fell heavily. Over the next several days, the pair got hit by 100-mile-per-hour windblasts and seven avalanches. Nyman managed to dig them out each time, but much of their equipment vanished in the snow. They had lost their ice axes and crampons by the time yet another avalanche sent them into a crevasse. Sweeney landed on a ledge as Nyman spread his own legs to brace himself against the sides of a funnel that led to an abyss. Fortunately the walls of the crevasse were made of hard snow, enabling Nyman to climb out—towing his partner by clenching the rope between his teeth. Eight days after Sweeney's initial fall, the companions made it off the mountain, reaching the Ruth Glacier. The weather lifted just long enough for a rescue plane to spot them, exposed and exhausted on the ice.

Expert Advice: When climbing in a national park, always take a radio tuned to a channel monitored by wardens.

HOW TO MAKE AN EMERGENCY SLED OUT OF ROPE AND SKIS

1 Unfurl the rope on the ground.
One hundred feet of rope at least half an inch in diameter should be adequate, but the longer, the better.

2 Bend the rope to form the bottom of the stretcher.
Beginning at the center of the rope and working outward in both directions, turn the rope into a series of S-curves. The segments of rope between the turns will be close together and parallel to one another, forming the bed of the stretcher. Allow enough space between each fold to accommodate the width of the person you must carry. The bed will consist of 16 parallel segments of rope with at least 20 feet of slack trailing off from either end.

3 Use the slack to tie a clove hitch at each turn, forming a series of loops at the sides of the stretcher.
To tie a clove hitch, encircle one of the curves you created in step 2 with the end of the rope. Bring the end around the curve again to encircle the curve in the rope a second time, then tuck the end through the second circle, choking the curve in the rope into a loop. Pull to tighten. The knots can be adjusted for tightness at a later stage. Thread the extra slack through the loops you've just created.

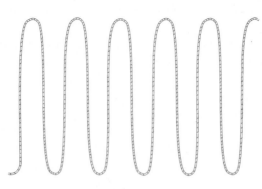

*Turn the rope into a series of S-curves,
starting at the rope's midpoint.*

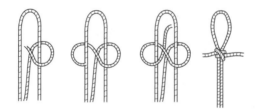

Tie a clove-hitch knot around the S-curves to form loops.

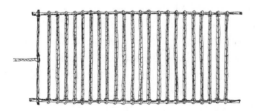

*Add branches for stability. Lash skis under the sled for
increased mobility and a smoother ride.*

4 Thread a sapling through the loops at either side of the stretcher.
Use two thin, sturdy saplings or tree branches about as wide as the skis they'll be mounted upon.

5 Tighten the knots around the saplings.
The saplings should remain parallel to one another.

6 Secure the saplings on top of the skis.
Use smaller pieces of rope, duct tape, backpack straps/webbing, or a strong fabric torn from expendable clothing to attach the saplings to the skis, keeping the bottom of the skis as smooth as possible.

7 Lash a pair of shorter branches across the front and back ends of the sled to increase stability.

8 Tie a length of rope to the front end as a towing cable.
If you have no rope left, pull out some of the extra slack from the loops on the side of the stretcher.

9 Place the victim on the stretcher.
Clothe the victim in as many layers as possible before setting him upon the stretcher. Secure him to the stretcher with extra rope or some of the slack from the loops on the side of the stretcher. Pull on the tow cord to haul the sled behind you on flat terrain. Proceed with caution over slopes, holding the tow cord from an uphill position.

Avalanche Alert

* **Wear an avalanche cord in dangerous terrain.** An avalanche cord is a thin, brightly colored strip of nylon that drags behind you as you walk. In the event of an avalanche, the light cord is more likely to stay near the surface, helping rescuers to spot you—especially if a helium-filled balloon is attached to the cord.

* **If you are caught in an avalanche, stay atop the snow with swimming strokes.** Face down the mountain and move your arms as if you were swimming freestyle, to keep your head above the tumbling snow.

* **If you are buried, dig your way out.** Determine which way is up by letting drool fall from your mouth. Dig in the opposite direction quickly but without panicking.

* **Once you are on the surface, look for trapped companions near obstacles.** Areas near trees or other natural barriers are the most likely places for your companions to be buried. Look for signs of movement before digging with a rescue shovel, to minimize your time in dangerous terrain—one avalanche can often set the stage for another.

///

CONTACT LENSES AT ALTITUDE

Hiking and climbing at high elevations make contact lenses problematic. Soft contact lenses reduce the amount of oxygen available to the cornea, and wearing extended-use contacts at high altitude increases the risk of corneal ulcers. When hiking above 8,000 feet, do not wear extended-use lenses for more than seven days in a row. Lens solution may freeze solid overnight; keep eye-moisture solutions liquid by carrying them close to your body. Always bring sunglasses and tinted backup eyeglasses.

MOUNTAIN INSOMNIA

Sleep trouble is common at high elevations, but do not take sleeping pills to help you through the night. Tranquilizer medications increase the risk of acute mountain sickness.

TRAVERSING SNOW IN HIGH ALTITUDES

- Snow crusts are at their strongest early in the morning.
- Areas around tree trunks and boulders may contain empty cavities beneath a thin layer of surface snow.
- Dirty snow absorbs more heat and therefore tends to be firmer than nearby clean snow.
- In the northern hemisphere, south- and west-facing slopes tend to have firmer snow than north- and east-facing slopes.

///

COOKING AT ALTITUDE

Because atmospheric pressure decreases at high elevations, water boils at a lower temperature*, extending the time it takes to cook food.

Elevation	Boiling Point	Cooking Time Equivalent to 1 Minute at Sea Level
5,000 feet	203°F	2 minutes
10,000 feet	194°F	4 minutes
15,000 feet	185°F	7 minutes
20,000 feet	176°F	13 minutes

*At sea level, water boils at 212°F.

Out and About

Avalanches are most likely when:

- a slope is angled between 30 and 50 degrees
- a slope has a convex shape
- a slope is permanently shaded from the sun
- there are no trees or natural obstacles to anchor snow
- new snow falls quickly on existing snow
- high winds prevent snow particles from bonding to one another
- the air temperature rises rapidly
- rain falls on existing snow

OLYMPIC HOCKEY PLAYER TAKES WRONG TURN ON MOUNTAIN

As the sun went down on California's Mammoth Mountain, snowboarder Eric LeMarque realized he was lost. In a desperate attempt to speed himself to civilization and safety, he snapped his boots into his snowboard and raced down the mountain slope—in the wrong direction. The former Olympic hockey player was not prepared for extended time in the wilderness; his survival gear was limited to a pack of soggy matches, a cell phone with a dead battery, and four sticks of gum. After shivering through the night alone, he continued in the wrong direction the next day. Realizing he was making no progress, he tuned his MP3 player to a radio broadcast from the nearby town of Mammoth, reasoning that the signal would come through best when he pointed it in that direction. Armed with this assumption, he changed course, using the MP3 player like a sonic compass—but he had wandered too far off course initially for the change in direction to offer immediate results. The second night he used the blade of his snowboard to chop enough pine branches for a bed to elevate his body from the frozen snow. He ate pine seeds and tree bark for nourishment. Five days after getting lost, he ran out of steam and hunkered down in a snow shelter on a part of the mountain where he could be spotted by rescuers. Two days later, an Army National Guard helicopter crew spotted him with an infrared optical device. The 34-year-old had lost 35 pounds in one week and would soon lose both his feet to amputation—but doctors were able to save his life.

Expert Advice: When you realize you are lost, make a plan before you act. Acting rashly and putting more distance between yourself and safety will minimize your chances of survival.

TEN MUST-HAVE ITEMS IN THE MOUNTAINS

1. **Compass:** For navigation
2. **Rope:** For climbing, shelter construction, emergency stretchers
3. **Knife:** For gathering food, protection
4. **Sunglasses:** Protect eyes from snow blindness and freezing wind
5. **Lighter:** More reliable than matches for lighting fires, melting snow for water
6. **Extra bootlaces:** For replacing a broken lace, binding sticks or logs to make shelter or raft
7. **Duct tape:** For fixing broken equipment, bandaging a flesh wound
8. **Four-season tent:** Bringing shelter is easier than making it
9. **Sleeping pad:** Insulates body from freezing ground, preventing hypothermia
10. **Waterproof and windproof outer shell:** Conserves body heat

MYTH: You can prevent altitude sickness by being in top physical condition.

FACT: The human body's response to elevation gains is basically the same no matter how much cardiovascular training a person has undergone. The slower progress of a moderately fit person actually can serve as a natural guard against altitude sickness—trekkers who are extremely physically fit are more likely to succumb to the temptation to ascend too far, too quickly.

HOW TO BREAK A TRAIL IN WAIST-DEEP SNOW

⭐ Read the terrain before choosing a route.
In the mountains, perfectly flat expanses of snow can indicate a body of water underneath. Where possible, follow a path made up of slight inclines next to steeper slopes, to minimize the possibility of traversing incompletely frozen ponds or lakes. Never walk within 5 feet of a precipice, as snow can drift to form unstable cornices that overhang solid ground by several feet.

⭐ Favor hard snow.
Hard snow tends to be shiny, with light reflecting off its upper crust. It will bear your weight better than soft, powdery snow.

⭐ Make your footprint bigger to minimize sinking.
Wear snowshoes or wrap rags and bundles of sticks around your legs. If you don't have snowshoes and cannot locate natural materials to make your own, wrap your legs in extra clothes, a torn tarp, or another material that will help prevent your pants from becoming waterlogged, which would increase the potential for frostbite and hypothermia.

*Tamp the snow forcefully with your feet to make
the trail more permanent.*

✪ Use walking poles or a stick to probe the ground in front of you.
If the tips break through ice, walk backward several paces, retracing your footsteps. Survey your surroundings, then choose another route.

✪ Take small steps.
As you progress, tamp down the snow forcefully with your feet and knees to make the trail more permanent.

✪ When in a group, walk in a single-file line.
Because breaking trail requires far more energy than walking over a firm path, share the effort by rotating the leader to the back of the line every 15 minutes. Switching frequently will minimize water lost through perspiration by any one member of the group, ultimately conserving fluids for all and preventing unwanted sweat from cooling the body too rapidly.

How to Make an Improvised Snowshoe

1 Bend a flexible sapling into a large teardrop shape.
Secure the ends to one another by lashing them with string, duct tape, or an extra bootlace.

2 Bind three sets of three sticks together.
Find sticks slightly longer than the width of the teardrop, then tape or tie them together in sets of three.

3 Lash the crossing sticks to the teardrop frame.
Situate the bundles of sticks so they are parallel to one another, making a ladder across the frame.

4 Anchor your boot into the frame.
Tie string across each shoe, securing it to each bundle of sticks where it overlaps the frame. Tie the rear line around your ankle for additional support.

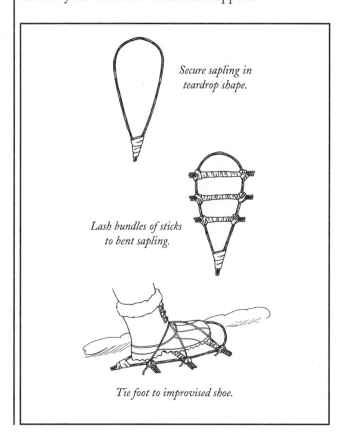

Secure sapling in teardrop shape.

Lash bundles of sticks to bent sapling.

Tie foot to improvised shoe.

THE SEVEN SUMMITS

When considered together, the highest peaks on each of the continental plates are called the Seven Summits. Only the most elite mountain climbers have conquered them all.

Continent	Mountain	Location	Height (in feet)
Asia	Mount Everest	Nepal/Tibet	29,035
South America	Aconcagua	Argentina	22,840
North America	Mount McKinley (a.k.a. Denali)	Alaska	20,320
Africa	Kilimanjaro	Tanzania	19,339
Europe	Mount Elbrus	Russia	18,481
Antarctica	Vinson Massif	Antarctica	16,067
Australasia*	Carstensz Pyramid	Indonesia	16,023
	Mount Kosciuszko	Australia	7,310

* Some climbers identify Australia's Mt. Kosciuszko as one of the seven, while others argue for Indonesia's more challenging Carstensz Pyramid.

HIKER PERSEVERES 40 DAYS WITHOUT FOOD

As James Scott attempted to cross a 14,000-foot Himalayan pass in December 1991, a blizzard obscured the trail he was following. Lost on the mountainside, Scott turned back, reasoning that a creek he found would eventually lead him to a village. Instead, he arrived at a dead end when the creek plummeted over the mountainside in a daunting waterfall. The 22-year-old trekker took shelter beneath a rock overhang for the night, then continued through the snow the next morning. Again he failed to reach the settlement on his map, but now he was completely out of water and limited to just two chocolate bars for sustenance. Scott hunkered down beneath a slim rock ledge and ate the last of his food. The next day, exhausted, he reached the rock overhang that became his shelter for the next 40 days. With the exception of one set of clothing and his sleeping bag, everything in his rucksack had gotten soaked in a creek the previous day. It took two weeks for him to dry out his belongings in the frigid air. Meanwhile he made snowballs and let them melt in the sun, sucking out the water little by little. With the exception of a single caterpillar, he ingested no food. Though his muscles atrophied and movement was difficult, thoughts of his family and fiancée kept him from abandoning hope of rescue. Finally, after 42 days of solitude, a helicopter spotted him in a nearby clearing and he was airlifted to a hospital to regain his strength.

Expert Advice: In extreme conditions, the human body is much better able to survive for long periods without food than without shelter. When lost in the mountains, locate a safe, dry place to take refuge before exhaustion overwhelms you.

MOUNT EVEREST
"The Third Pole"

BEST KNOWN FOR: Being the tallest mountain on Earth

LOCATION: Himalayan mountain range, on the border of Nepal and Tibet

HEIGHT: 29,035 feet

DANGERS: Oxygen levels at summit 65% lower than at sea level • Rapid weather changes • Shifting terrain and hidden crevasses of the Khumbu Icefall at the mountain's base • The Lhotse Wall's 4,000-foot ice slope • The Death Zone, the area above 26,000 feet • Vertical climb at 28,800 feet, highest technical climbing in the world

LITTLE-KNOWN FACT: In 2003, the Coalition for Texans with Disabilities organized a successful trek to Everest Base Camp that included a paralytic and a man in a wheelchair.

Lowest temperature at summit: -70°F • Highest recorded wind speed: 150 miles per hour • Climbing deaths: 189 • Deadliest year: 1996, 15 deaths • First to summit: Sir Edmund Hillary and Tenzing Norgay Sherpa, 1953 • First to summit without oxygen tanks: Reinhold Messner and Peter Habeler, 1978 • Most personal summits: Apa Sherpa, 16 • Fastest climb from base camp to summit: Pemba Dorjee Sherpa, 8 hours 10 minutes

///

HOW TO AVOID THE "KHUMBU COUGH"

The extremely low humidity at high elevations irritates the respiratory system, potentially producing coughs violent enough to fracture ribs. The best way to prevent the "Khumbu Cough" is to breathe through a mask or layers of fabric that will heat and moisten the air you breathe, both during the day and overnight.

///

HEIGHT OF MOUNT EVEREST

MOUNT EVEREST   MATTERHORN   MOUNT RAINIER   MOUNT FUJI

Mount Everest	29,035 feet
Matterhorn	14,693 feet
Mount Rainier	14,410 feet
Mount Fuji	12,388 feet

HERZOG SETS CLIMBING RECORD, LOSES FINGERS AND TOES

Soon after becoming the first men to summit any of the world's 8,000-meter peaks on June 3, 1950, Maurice Herzog and Louis Lachenal experienced the perils of oxygen deprivation on Nepal's Annapurna. When Herzog's gloves went tumbling down the mountain in a moment of carelessness, he continued his descent gloveless, forgetting that he'd brought along an extra pair of socks for just such an emergency. By the time the men arrived at the high camp established by two support climbers, Herzog's fingers were as stiff as wood, and Lachenal's feet were badly frostbitten. After a hellish, stormy night, the reunited team lost their way while descending to the next camp down. Their cries for help went unanswered, and darkness fell. Lachenal plunged into a crevasse, disappearing. Facing death unless they found a shelter, the other men followed him down the icy tunnel into a space just large enough for all of them. They removed their boots and huddled together for the night. In the morning they discovered that an avalanche had shot down the chute and covered everything. By the time Herzog and Lachenal located their boots, Herzog's fingers were so numb and both of their feet so swollen that they couldn't put them back on. Meanwhile, the two support climbers had gone completely snowblind. Back out on the mountain face, one of the blind men put Lachenal's feet in his boots and later did the same for Herzog, cutting the uppers with a knife to slide them on. As Herzog reconciled himself to death, he saw a fifth support climber making his way over the snow in his direction. His fingers and toes would soon be amputated, but the team had made it just far enough to survive.

Expert Advice: Keep emergency equipment and clothing in an obvious and easily accessible part of your pack.

High-Altitude Illnesses

Illness	Symptoms	Treatment
Mild Acute Mountain Sickness	Headache, dizziness, and nausea during first 12 hours in high altitude	Descend 1,500 feet or more and wait for body to acclimatize
Moderate Acute Mountain Sickness	Bad headache, nausea, dizziness, insomnia, fatigue, and fluid retention after 12 hours at high altitude	Descend at least 1,500 feet; take oxygen if possible
High-Altitude Cerebral Edema	Acute headache, nausea, dizziness, and fatigue for 24 hours; mental confusion; clumsiness and lack of muscle coordination	Take oxygen; descend immediately; evacuate the mountain or use a portable hyperbaric chamber; take dexamethasone and/or acetazolamide
High-Altitude Pulmonary Edema	Moist cough, shortness of breath, rapid breathing, severe weakness and drowsiness, rapid heartbeat, bluish skin	Take oxygen; descend as soon as possible; use a portable hyperbaric chamber; take nifedipine
High-Altitude Retinal Hemorrhage (bleeding in retina)	Blind spots; if bleeding is light, may have no symptoms	Descend immediately if blind spots develop. Problem typically resolves itself 2 to 8 weeks after occurrence

MOST DANGEROUS HIMALAYAN PEAKS

Mountain	Altitude	Recorded Summits	Deaths	Fatality Rate
Annapurna	26,539 feet	130	53	41%
Nanga Parbat	26,650 feet	216	61	28%
K2	28,244 feet	198	53	27%
Kanchenjunga	28,162 feet	185	40	22%
Manaslu	26,775 feet	240	52	22%
Dhaulagiri	26,818 feet	313	56	18%
Makalu	27,831 feet	206	22	11%
Gasherbrum	26,503 feet	195	21	11%
Shisha Pangma	26,329 feet	201	19	9%
Everest	29,035 feet	2,800+	189	6%

//

ADJUSTING TO HIGHER ALTITUDES

Giving your body time to adjust to the reduced oxygen in the air as you move into higher elevations is the best way to avoid high-altitude illnesses. When hiking at altitudes greater than 8,000 meters, sleep at an altitude of no more than 1,000 meters higher than you slept the night before. For every three consecutive days of 1,000-meter elevation gains, rest an extra day and night before ascending farther. Drinking at least four liters of fluids a day will help you acclimatize.

//

K2

"The Savage Mountain"

BEST KNOWN FOR: Being harder to climb than Mount Everest

LOCATION: Karakoram range in the Himalayas, on the border of Pakistan and China; so remote that you must either hike 40 miles up the Baltoro Glacier in northern Pakistan or fly to Islamabad, drive 500 miles northeast into China, travel by jeep across the Taklimakan Desert, then caravan by camel to reach the base of the mountain range

HEIGHT: 28,244 feet

DANGERS: Descent so perilous that 1 in 7 of those who summit die on the way down • Oxygen levels 65% lower than at sea level • Weather far more unpredictable and vicious than Everest • So remote that helicopters are unable to reach base camp for rescue operations • Climbing next to the fragile columns of ice of the "Bottleneck" couloir (gully) below the summit

LITTLE-KNOWN FACT: Twenty-three years after the first successful summit of K2, a Japanese team used 1,500 porters to become the second group to the top.

First to summit: Lino Lacedelli and Achille Compagnoni, 1954 • Most famous Satanist to attempt a summit: Aleister Crowley, 1902 • Deadliest wind: A 1995 gale that blew Alison Hargreaves and five other climbers off the mountaintop on a clear day

CLIMBER SURVIVES FALL AFTER PARTNER CUTS ROPE

After reaching the summit of Peru's Siula Grande in 1985, Joe Simpson slipped on a steep ice patch and fell hard, driving his tibia through his kneecap. Unable to walk, his only hope lay in his partner, Simon Yates. The pair were out of water and cooking fuel and needed to descend the mountain as quickly as possible. Their plan was to tie themselves to either end of a rope and for Yates to dig in to the snow and lower his partner down 300 feet at a time. Yates would then climb down after him, repeating the exercise until they hit bottom. After several successful iterations, Yates let out his rope as he had been doing, but this time he never felt Simpson signal that he was secure. Yates had unwittingly lowered his partner into a crevasse, where Simpson dangled in midair. Unsure of what had happened, Yates waited for an hour as Simpson's weight on the other end of the rope weakened his hold on the snowy mountainside. Finally, facing certain catastrophe, he cut the rope, dropping Simpson into a crevasse the size of St. Peter's cathedral in Rome. Incredibly, Simpson survived the fall. There was no way for him to climb out of the deep crevasse, so as Yates descended the mountain the long way, certain his friend was dead, Simpson anchored the rope and, despite his broken knee, rappelled even deeper into the crevasse. The crevasse led to the treacherous glacier at the mountain's base, over which Simpson hobbled and crawled for four days until he reached Yates' tent—just hours before Yates had planned to hike out without him.

Expert Advice: Most climbing accidents happen on the way down the mountain. If an ascent is taking longer than expected, creating the need to hurry and depleting your provisions, consider turning back and attempting to summit another time.

HOW TO SURVIVE A LIGHTNING STORM ON A MOUNTAINSIDE

1 Recognize the signs of an approaching storm.

Typical visual cues like cloud cover and light flashes may be obscured by the terrain, tree cover, or your location. Other signs of electrical storms include the smell of ozone, a buzzing sound in the air, or hair that stands up straight. A halo of light known as St. Elmo's fire may be apparent around trees or people.

2 Break away from the group.

If everyone gets struck at once, no one will be able to help the victims.

3 Remove any jewelry or metal on your body.

If your backpack has a metal frame, take off the backpack.

4 Seek a dry, safe shelter.

If you are surrounded by trees, position yourself among the shortest trees in the vicinity. Stay away from trees scarred by previous lightning strikes. If the mountainside is bare, retreat to a lower position if there is time. Avoid overhangs and ridgelines. Try to find a slight bump in the mountainside that will elevate you—but only slightly—from the path electricity will likely travel if lightning strikes the ground nearby. A dry cave that is deeper than its mouth is wide is also a good location to wait out the storm.

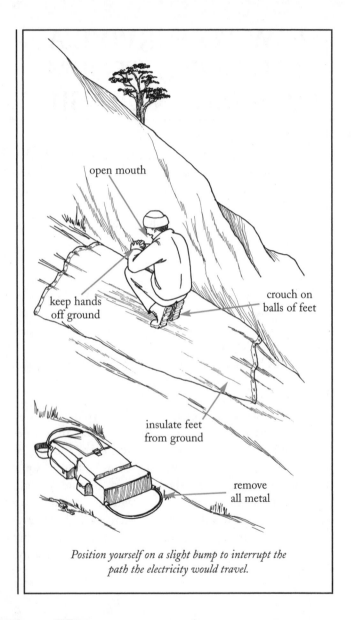

open mouth

keep hands
off ground

crouch on
balls of feet

insulate feet
from ground

remove
all metal

*Position yourself on a slight bump to interrupt the
path the electricity would travel.*

5 Separate yourself from the ground.

Place insulators like wood, rubber, plastic, or natural (not synthetic) cloth on the ground in your sheltered location.

6 Make yourself as small a target as possible.

Crouch on the balls of your feet on top of the insulation. Put your head down and keep your mouth open to protect your eardrums. Do not put your hands on the ground.

7 After the storm passes, assess whether anyone in your group has been hit.

Common indications that someone has been struck by lightning include temporary hearing loss, dilated pupils, amnesia, paralysis, confusion, weak pulse at the extremities, and irregular heartbeat. If the victim is unconscious, make sure he or she is breathing and perform CPR if necessary. Seek medical attention as soon as possible.

TURTLE MOUNTAIN COLLAPSE CRUSHES VALLEY UNDER 80 MILLION TONS OF LIMESTONE

Just before the ceilings in the mine started to collapse, coalminer Dan McKenzie heard a thunderous cracking sound high above him. At 4:10 A.M. on April 29, 1903, McKenzie was halfway through the nightshift inside Turtle Mountain in the Canadian Rockies when a massive piece of the mountain's eastern slope broke off. It slid 2,300 feet down the mountainside, spreading limestone, mud, and sludge into a 1.2-mile area of the Crowsnest Valley and trapping at least 100 citizens under the rubble in the small town of Frank, Alberta. In the aftermath of the slide, McKenzie regained his composure and ran for the mine's entrance, but he and the 16 other miners who gathered there discovered they were trapped. The men started digging at the blocked entrance, but the more they hammered, the more rubble fell in their path. McKenzie set out to explore other parts of the mine and returned to confirm their worst fears—the fresh-air shafts had been sealed in the rockslide, meaning they had limited time to escape before they suffocated. The men transferred their escape efforts to a vertical coal shaft deeper inside the mine, and after digging for hours, their oxygen dwindling and exhaustion setting in, McKenzie broke through to the outside. A stream of light shone on the miners and fresh air rushed into the shaft. The miners soon discovered that the location of their tunnel was too dangerous to climb out of—it was directly in the path of a stream of rocks that continued to tumble down the mountain—but with buoyed spirits they dug another tunnel nearby. The exit of the new tunnel was protected by a large boulder, and all 17 of the miners safely emerged from the mountain 13 hours after the slide.

Expert Advice: If you are caught below falling rocks on a mountainside, seek shelter behind a rock outcropping or an embedded boulder. Crouch into a ball with your hands protecting your head.

WORLD'S DEEPEST CANYONS

Continent	Name	Location	Maximum Depth
Asia	Yarlung Tsangpo	Tibet	16,650 feet
South America	Cotahuasi	Peru	11,000 feet
North America	Hells Canyon	Idaho	7,913 feet
Europe	Tara Canyon	Montenegro	5,000 feet
Africa	Blyde River Canyon	South Africa	2,790 feet
Australasia	Kings Canyon	Australia	885 feet

Out and About

The standard international system for rating rapids features six categories, ranging from light riffles (Class I) to unrunnable whitewater (Class VI). However, the Grand Canyon still rates its rapids with an older system that ranges from 1 to 10. Many rafters just divide these ratings by 2 to estimate the standard international rating. The biggest rapids in the Grand Canyon generally fall into the Class V category.

ONE-ARMED MAJOR COMMANDS FIRST KNOWN MISSION THROUGH GRAND CANYON

Having lost his right arm during the American Civil War, Major John Wesley Powell seemed an unlikely leader for a scouting mission through the Grand Canyon. But on May 24, 1869, he directed the four boats that set off on an expedition the local Native American tribes considered so treacherous as to be impossible. By the time the boats reached Utah, the churning rapids and dangerous portages had already destroyed one boat, washed away numerous supplies and provisions, and convinced the first of several men to quit before they'd even entered the most perilous phase of the journey. As the remaining group proceeded into the canyon, Powell often played the role of scout, climbing up the riverbanks to see what hazards lay on the river ahead. On one occasion, he used his one good arm to scale a cliff and found himself at an impasse just below the top. There was no way to go up, and the only way down involved releasing his grasp before his foot could make contact with a toehold. One of his compatriots had managed to reach a ledge above, but there was no stick to lower down to Powell and the weakening ground beneath Powell's feet afforded no time to fetch rope from the boats. Thinking quickly, the man tore off his pants and dangled them over the edge. Powell felt the fabric brush against his hand, let go of the cliff, and grabbed for his life, catching the pant leg and scrambling to safety. On August 29, Powell and his men made it through the Grand Canyon, becoming the first known people to do so.

Expert Advice: Never enter a river gorge on a raft without scouting first. If climbing may be necessary, equip yourself with rope before setting out.

HOW TO RUN THE COLORADO RIVER THROUGH THE GRAND CANYON WITHOUT A GUIDE

⭐ Read the rapids.
Look for a V-shaped pattern of ripples that points downstream into the churning waves. This is usually where the water is deepest and fastest, reducing the potential for collision with an underwater rock. With your boat facing straight ahead, paddle into the current that will naturally lead you to the middle of the V.

⭐ Paddle furiously.
Hit the whitewater with as much speed as possible. The bigger the waves, the more important it is to paddle hard and maintain momentum as you pass over them. If the raft is moving too slowly, it may slide backward over a standing wave and get stuck or capsize.

⭐ Use the weight of the rafters to propel the raft forward.
Roiling water will spin the raft sideways, causing it to lose momentum. Quickly move all the passengers to the side of the raft that has been thrown up into the air by a wave. If the raft loses forward momentum altogether, stay on the high side of the raft and use paddle strokes to pull the boat out of the hole.

★ If you get tossed overboard, attempt to get back in the boat.

Grab for another rafter's forearm with one hand and a rope on the side of the boat with the other.

★ If you can't get back in the boat, point your feet downstream and assume a sitting position.

Bend your knees, and bring your toes above the surface. Watch the boat and maneuver yourself so you don't come between it and a boulder. Resist the urge to stand up, which will likely result in the current hurling you dangerously forward. Avoid fallen trees, which can force a swimmer beneath the surface. At the end of the rapid, get back onto the nearest boat or swim to the shore as soon as possible.

★ If the boat flips, let your life preserver bring you to the surface.

If you come up beneath the raft, use your hands to move to one side. If there is no serious danger downstream, hold on to the raft on the upstream side, then climb on top of the overturned raft. If there are serious hazards downstream, move away from the raft and swim the rapid on your own, as described above. Once you reach placid water, bring the boat to the shore, turn it over, and assess your losses.

Point your feet downstream.

⭐ Use eddies to your advantage.

Between rapids, maneuver the raft into the gentle swirling currents and still spots commonly found at the river's edge to give yourself a chance to recuperate, scout the next rapid, and formulate a plan.

Be Aware

- The National Park Service requires all rafters to acquire a permit before taking a boat through the Grand Canyon. Noncommercial rafting permits are issued by lottery to experienced river rafters who choose not to hire a guide. Apply for your permit at least a year in advance; the waiting list for the lottery system can be as long as 10 years.

- Trips through the Grand Canyon can last as long as 25 days. All drinking water should be purified and all food waste must be carried out of the canyon.

- The National Park Service requires every person to have a life preserver and an oar. Each party is required to carry one extra life preserver for every ten rafters; a first aid kit; a signal mirror and two orange panels measuring 3 by 10 feet for forming an X visible to passing aircraft; two extra oars for each boat; a pump; detailed maps of the river. Because all human waste must be packed and carried out of the canyon, each party must also bring a portable toilet system.

- Helicopter evacuations are available for medical emergencies. The emergency radio channel is 121.50 MHz. A satellite telephone is recommended, as cell phone reception is unreliable or nonexistent inside the canyon. The emergency telephone number is (928) 638-7911.
- Before launching, make a note of the extended weather forecast and get an up-to-date schedule of dam releases. Flash floods caused by rain are the biggest danger in the Grand Canyon.
- The logistics of rafting the Grand Canyon can be almost as daunting as the whitewater. Planning 16 days of food for 16 people is a tall order, as is gathering all the proper equipment. Choose your river companions well; your safety will be in their hands.

CHAPTER 2
THE DESERT

YEAH, BUT IT'S A DRY HEAT

Ten Must-Have Items in the Desert

1. **Water:** One gallon per person, per day
2. **Pocket knife:** For whittling, cutting rope, cutting cactus
3. **Tarp:** For making shelter or shade, freeing car from sand, extra cover on cold night
4. **Signaling mirror:** For beckoning airplanes
5. **Matches:** For lighting fire to cook, heat, ward off animals
6. **Rope:** For safety when climbing in canyons or navigating cliffs
7. **Flashlight:** For identifying rodent warrens when animals come out at night
8. **Iodine:** For purifying standing water (if you find some)
9. **Black tea:** For soothing sunburns
10. **Pocket comb:** For removing cactus needles without sticking fingers

Out and About

The desert marshes, pools, and streams of the American Southwest are home to the astounding desert pupfish, which can survive water temperatures ranging from 40 to 112°F and salinity levels three times that of the ocean. Found in water as shallow as one inch, they often burrow into the underlying mud when temperatures drop.

HIKER AMPUTATES OWN ARM TO ESCAPE BOULDER

In late April 2003, 27-year-old Aron Ralston was hiking alone in the desert of eastern Utah when a boulder weighing more than 800 pounds fell on him. Unable to extricate his right arm, he spent hours trying to dislodge the boulder, chipping away at it with his multiuse tool and rigging a makeshift pulley system with his climbing gear. Nothing worked. He cried out for help, but the three-foot-wide slot canyon he had been exploring wasn't frequently visited, and since Ralston hadn't told anyone where he was planning to hike, he had little chance of being rescued. Four days passed. Ralston began saving his urine so he could drink it when he ran out of water. With his right hand already grayish blue and decomposing, Ralston realized that his last chance for survival was to amputate part of his arm. He used the elastic insulation tube from his empty water bottle as a tourniquet and unfolded the small blade from his multiuse tool. He cut away at his arm, hallucinating and drifting in and out of consciousness as he worked. Despite his success at severing several tendons, he was unable to saw through bone. On his sixth morning in the canyon, Ralston's hallucinations stopped just long enough for an epiphany: he could break his arm bones if he could create enough torque. Pushing on the boulder with his free hand and using his body weight, Ralston increased pressure until finally his bones snapped. After cutting through what remained of his forearm, he used his good arm to secure a rope and rappel down the canyon, where he was finally rescued by passing hikers.

Expert Advice: Even if you are an experienced hiker or climber, always hike with a companion or tell someone your route before you head out into the wilderness.

DEATH VALLEY

BEST KNOWN FOR: Extreme temperatures • Extreme drop in elevation, from a high point of 11,049 feet to a low point of 282 feet below sea level in a distance of less than 20 miles • Imperiling the lives of pioneers during the 1849 gold rush

LOCATION: Great Basin and Mojave Desert, southeastern California

DANGERS: Abandoned mines • Sidewinder rattlesnakes • Flash floods • Unabated sun

LITTLE-KNOWN FACT: Borax was discovered and mined in Death Valley in the mid-nineteenth century.

Record high temperature: 134°F • Average daily high temperature: 90°F • Highest recorded ground temperature: 201°F • Record low temperature: 15°F • Average nightly low temperature: 62°F • Average rainfall: 1.92 inches per year • Lowest recorded rainfall: 0 inches (1929) • Longest hot spell: 154 consecutive days above 100°F (2001) • Most common causes of death and injury: Car accidents, flash floods • Safest mode of travel: A well-stocked four-wheel-drive enclosed vehicle

HOW TO FREE A VEHICLE MIRED IN SOFT SAND

1 Determine an escape route.

Read the sand around you to establish the path on which you will be least likely to get stuck again. Look for sand with a pale yellow hue, indicating a coarse grain, and a rippled surface. Avoid tracts of golden red sand, which consists of fine particles through which traction is difficult to maintain; smooth tracts of sand, which can indicate a fresher, looser makeup; and the hollows between two dunes, which typically collect loose, powdery sand that offers little traction.

2 Dig.

Using a shovel, an empty cup or wide-mouthed container, or your hands, remove the soft sand from beneath the undercarriage of your vehicle, forming a gradual downward slope toward the direction of escape. Point the front wheels straight ahead.

3 Build a ramp.

Place long lengths of steel, aluminum, or wood under or against the vehicle's wheels, leading down the slope you have created. If these materials are not available, use a canvas mat, floor mats, tenting materials, or even a pair of denim pants—anything that will increase traction. If material is limited, place it beneath whichever pair of wheels is powered by the engine.

*Lay cloth, metal, or wood in front of the front wheels
to increase traction.*

4 Adjust the tire pressure.

If it is possible to let air out of the tires without lowering the undercarriage into the sand, do so to increase traction.

5 Start moving.

When the wheels gain traction on the metal, wooden, or canvas channels you have created, slowly accelerate to pick up speed.

6 Maintain your speed.

Don't stop. If the car or truck falters before you reach firmer ground, it will get stuck again.

Be Aware

Cars and trucks moving over dunes tend to whip up the top layer of sand, making it less firm. Virgin sand usually affords better traction. If you are traveling in a convoy and there is no known danger of landmines, make your own tracks instead of following behind the other vehicles in single file. Four-wheel-drive vehicles are the preferred mode of transport in desert terrain.

Out and About

Northern China's Badain Jaran Desert is home to the world's tallest sand dunes—at more than 1,600 feet tall, their ability to withstand the area's ferocious winds puzzled scientists for years. But in 2004, a researcher found water in one of the dunes after digging just six inches below the surface. A three-foot hole produced a small pool of water that defied the laws of nature—not only was the water coming from inside a desert dune, it was also 50 feet above the surface of a nearby lake, and therefore 50 feet above what was thought to be the natural water level. That water comes from the snowmelt of a mountain range 300 miles away, slowly making its way to the dune system, where it cements grains of sand together and prevents the wind from carrying the particles away. The scientists calculated that 500 million cubic meters of water pass through the vicinity every year, enough to supply a city of one million residents.

Out and About

In recent years strong winds of the Gobi Desert have blown countless tons of sand ever closer to China's capital, Beijing. Deserts less than 100 miles from the city are moving toward it at a rate of 2 miles per year, and the city itself experiences frequent sandstorms every spring that cover the city in a dusty haze. Great curtains of sand can extend up to 7 miles into the air, where high-altitude rivers of wind carry the sand all the way across the Pacific Ocean to North America. The problem has been exacerbated by deforestation. In response, Chinese officials have launched a massive tree-planting effort, hoping that a "Great Green Wall" will stop the desert's advance.

DESERT TYPES

Type	Cause of Dryness	Typical Location	Examples
Rain Shadow Desert	Storm systems hit mountain ranges and drop moisture on windward side of the slopes, leaving little rain for the other side	Leeward side of continental mountain ranges	Death Valley, California; Atacama, Chile
Coastal Desert	Cold ocean current hitting a coastline inhibits the formation of rain clouds, creating a landscape prone to desertification	Western edges of continents between the Tropic of Cancer and the Tropic of Capricorn	Baja peninsula, Mexico; Namib desert, Namibia
Remote Interior Basin	Land is so far from an ocean or lake that storm systems lose all moisture passing over	Deep inland	Sahara, Africa; Gobi, Asia

MYTH: Quicksand is a common hazard in the desert.

FACT: Quicksand is a mixture of fine-particle sand or silt, clay, and water—the last of which is rare in desert terrain. Quicksand is primarily found in marshes or near rivers and lakes. It also occurs in some ocean bays. Because the human body is typically less dense than quicksand, it tends to float on the surface, making quicksand less of a danger than a nuisance wherever it occurs.

GROUND SIGNALS FOR PASSING AIRCRAFT

Pilots can read these symbols and help accordingly.

F	Need food and water	**K**	Need to know which direction to proceed
X	Require medical assistance	**△**	Believed safe to land here
Y	Yes	**N**	No
I	Serious injury/Need doctor	**□**	Need compass and map
↑	Am traveling this way	**LL**	All is well
JL	Do not understand	**SOS**	International distress symbol

//

SIGNALING AIRCRAFTS

To bounce sunlight off a small mirror or wristwatch dial to signal a passing aircraft, hold one hand at arm's length from your face with two fingers spread into a V. Use your other hand to position your mirror just under one eye, facing away from you, and frame the helicopter or airplane between your two raised fingers. Swivel the mirror back and forth so that the reflected light jumps from one finger to another—as you do so, the light will hit the plane in the middle. Mirror signals can be seen for more than 100 miles in the desert.

//

Out and About

The deathstalker scorpion, found in the desert regions of North Africa and the Middle East, is the most venomous scorpion in the world. The four-inch-long arachnid can be identified by its thin yellow tail and narrow claws. Despite its name, the deathstalker doesn't usually kill humans with its sting, as it typically injects only a tiny amount of venom at a time—enough to cause extreme pain in adults and to endanger the lives of children. A different species holds the record for human deaths: the similarly sized fat-tail scorpion, a dark-colored scorpion that delivers enough venom in its sting to cause several human fatalities each year.

MYTH: Never drink alcoholic or caffeinated beverages in the desert.

FACT: Because drinks containing alcohol and caffeine have diuretic properties that can increase the urge to urinate, many believe that such beverages do more harm than good for someone struggling to survive in the desert. This is not always the case. Although the alcohol in beer spurs a brief diuretic effect, that relatively low alcohol content is outweighed by the benefits that the water in the beer can have on the body. And if you are accustomed to drinking caffeinated beverages regularly, your body will have adjusted itself to the presence of the chemical, minimizing the diuretic effect. If coffee or tea is a novelty to you, on the other hand, it may drive your fluid balance in the wrong direction and should be avoided.

HOW TO MAKE, AND COOK WITH, A PIT OVEN

1 Dig a hole.
In firm terrain, preferably in a natural depression, make a pit about three feet deep and three feet wide.

2 Cover the bottom of the hole with rocks.
Search for stones as big as grapefruits, and preferably flat. Lay them out in a solid layer. Set several rocks aside for later use.

3 Build a fire.
Collect wood and set it alight on top of the rocks in the bottom of the pit. Do not lean over the hole as the fire grows; the rocks may shoot out splinters as they heat up.

4 Spread the coals.
Using a thick branch or another long tool, scatter the burning coals evenly across the bottom of the pit.

5 Use more rocks to form a grate.
Arrange several large rocks in a square in the center of the coals.

6 Cook your food on the grate.
Rodents and lizards are all you are likely to find in the desert. To cook a lizard, make a cut from shoulder to

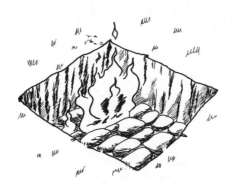

Build a fire on top of flat rocks in pit.

Spread coals, form a grate with more rocks,
and roast meat on spit.

shoulder and discard the head and neck; peel the skin off after cooking is complete. For rodents, use a knife to remove all hair and skin before cooking, as well as abdominal organs such as the stomach and intestines. Younger animals are more tender and therefore can be skewered on a stick and roasted; older animals will be better when stewed in boiling water. Drink the cooking water for additional nutrients.

7 Seal in the heat.
To make the meat cook faster, lay a dampened canvas tarp on top of the pit to trap the heat inside the oven. Set rocks around the perimeter of the tarp to keep it in place.

8 Cover the pit with sand when you are finished.
Shovel a pile of sand into the pit to cover the hot rocks before you leave the area.

EDIBLE PLANTS OF THE DESERT

Name	Characteristics	Edible Part	How to Eat
Acacia	Short tree; gray-white bark; small, alternating leaves; yellow ball-shaped flowers	Dark brown pods, flowers, young leaves	Raw
Agave	Cluster of long, fleshy green leaves radiating from a central stalk	Flowers, flower buds	Boil flowers and buds before eating
Amaranth	Tall, with alternating leaves; green flowers at top; brown/black seeds	Seeds, leaves	Seeds and leaves: raw; seeds: pound into flour
Date Palm	Tall tree with no branches; huge compound leaves at crown; yellow fruits	Fruits	Fresh or sun-dried
Prickly Pear Cactus	Thick stem; clustered pads covered with needles; red or yellow flowers; punctured pads seep non-milky juice	Fruits at the top of the stalks; the pads themselves	Fruit: raw; pads: remove thorns and nodes, peel, and boil or grill

MAN SPENDS 40 DAYS, 40 NIGHTS ALONE IN DESERT

On July 11, 1999, Robert Bogucki sent his parents a postcard announcing his intention to travel solo across Australia's Great Sandy Desert, a 160,000-square mile wilderness so barren that even the ever-resourceful Aborigines avoided it. And as a resident of Fairbanks, Alaska, the 33-year-old volunteer firefighter had little experience in desert survival. But despite the challenges he faced, Bogucki struck out alone on what he considered a spiritual quest. Two weeks later, tourists came across his bike and some camping gear. A rescue mission was mounted and trackers began following Bogucki's trail, but when they lost his tracks after a 180-mile search, the mission was called off and Bogucki presumed dead. His parents, however, refused to give up hope—they hired a private search-and-rescue team headed by American Garrison St. Clair. Eleven days after the initial search had ended, St. Clair and his associates headed into the desert with four-wheel-drive vehicles, a helicopter, dogs, and infrared goggles. Three days later, the helicopter spotted some of Bogucki's belongings, including a treasured Bible. Several miles away, the team found the man they were looking for in a dry creek bed. He had survived by eating plants and flowers and drinking muddy water, and claimed to have discovered the peace he had yearned for at the beginning of his journey. Even the timing of his rescue had a spiritual dimension for Bogucki—he said his trial in the desert had lasted 40 days and 40 nights.

Expert Advice: If you are wandering in the desert and wish to aid rescuers rather than evade them, leave nonessential belongings in conspicuous places to provide clues to your whereabouts.

//

DESERT HYGIENE

While traveling in the desert, all water you're carrying should be saved for drinking. If you have been in the desert long enough that your skin is on the verge of drying and cracking, potentially leading to infections, rub your body with gritty red sand. Reddish sands often contain iron ore, which has anti-bacterial properties that will keep your skin healthy.

STRANDED VEHICLE

If you are stranded in the desert in a car or a jeep, open its hood to signal distress to passing aircrafts and stay near the car rather than wandering off into the sand. Cars and jeeps are easier to spot from a distance than solitary human beings.

CONQUERING MIRAGES

Mirages are optical effects caused by the refraction of light through super-heated air. A mirage can make it difficult for observers to judge distance and identify objects, and can cause a rippling, illusionary effect that can be mistaken for a far-off stretch of water. If you are traveling through the desert and you think you've spotted an unexpected body of water in the distance, seek high ground or climb to the top of a dune. Raising your sightline as little as 10 feet above the hot, thick air at ground level can restore your ability to survey the landscape accurately. If high ground is unavailable, rest in the shade until the sun is setting or the moon is overhead, when the desert's features won't be obscured by heat.

//

MYTH: Camels carry water in their humps.

FACT: Camels' humps are fat depositories, serving both to store calories and to insulate the animal from the sun. It's the camel's digestive system that allows it to go for weeks without drinking. When a camel encounters water, it can take in as much as 50 gallons in less than two hours. Its digestive tract then releases the liquid slowly and without creating waste—their remarkable kidneys concentrate urine to the consistency of syrup, they rarely sweat, and their feces are so dry they can be used as fuel for fires as soon as the droppings hit the sand.

Out and About

The kangaroo rat has evolved an ideal desert survival strategy: the ability to live without ever drinking water. It makes its own moisture through a process in which oxygen taken in by the lungs metabolizes fats and starches, producing water within the body as a by-product. It also boasts nasal passageways that recycle the water vapor escaping its lungs when it breathes. Subsisting primarily on seeds, the kangaroo rat forages at night and spends its days in underground burrows whose entrances it blocks with dirt.

HOW TO KEEP BEVERAGES COLD IN THE DESERT

1 Dig a hole.
The hole should be deep enough that the tops of the beverages will be at least 1½ to 2 feet, and as far down as 4 to 5 feet below the surface. At about 2 feet below ground, the temperature will be about 30°F cooler than the surface. At about 5 feet, the temperature of the earth is consistently 50 to 55°F.

2 Wrap beverages in cloth.
Insulate the beverages by wrapping them in a blanket, tarp, or extra clothing to help maintain their chill.

3 Collect two flat boards.
Ideally, each board should be a foot longer and wider than the beverages. Allowing some air around the drinks adds a layer of cooling insulation.

4 Secure the beverages between the boards.
Use duct tape or rope to fasten the beverages between the boards.

5 Tie a rope around the boards.
The rope should be at least 4 feet longer than the hole is deep. Tie one end of the rope securely around the boards. Tie a flag or a colorful piece of cloth to the other end of the rope.

6   Lower the beverages into the hole.

7   Fill in the hole.
Keep the flag-end of the rope out of the hole so you will be able to find the spot where you buried the beverages when you're ready for a drink.

8   Tie the flag to a stick.
Raise the flag off the ground on a post or stick so it will not be buried beneath a layer of sand if the desert winds kick up. Make a mental note of other landmarks in the area, such as large rocks, cacti, or other vegetation.

Be Aware

In the extreme desert heat, conserve your energy by performing physical labor at night. If you must work in the daylight, do so in the early morning and late afternoon, when the shadows are longest and you can take best advantage of the shade they afford.

Sandwich beverages between two boards.

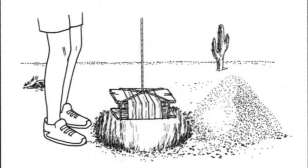

Lower beverages into hole.

Take careful note of the location.

RUNNER TAKES 130-MILE DETOUR THROUGH DESERT

In the 1994 Marathon des Sables, a six-day, 150-kilometer footrace across the Sahara in southern Morocco, Mauro Prosperi was in sixth place when he was caught in a sandstorm. Disoriented but undeterred, the Italian policeman kept running even though the course had disappeared in the sand. After running for several hours without seeing another participant, Prosperi realized he was in trouble. Like his fellow competitors, he was carrying enough food to get him to the finish line, but he was relying on the race organizers to provide water and shelter at predetermined resting points. Thirty-six hours after losing his way and wandering so far off course that he'd crossed the border into Algeria, he ran out of food and water. Prosperi stumbled into an abandoned mosque, where he took shelter and managed to kill and eat some of the bats and snakes living there. Giving up hope of rescue after several days, he resigned himself to death and attempted to minimize his suffering by slitting his wrists, but his extreme dehydration saved his life: the lack of water made the racer's blood so thick that it quickly clotted and sealed his wounds. Nine days after Prosperi deviated from the course, a group of nomads found him in the mosque, 130 miles away from the racecourse. They blindfolded him and took him to an Algerian military camp, from which he was transferred to a hospital. Though he lost 30 pounds and nearly suffered liver failure during his nine-day ordeal, Prosperi not only survived, but returned to compete again in 1998—only to be forced out by a badly stubbed toe.

Expert Advice: If you are caught in a sandstorm, mark your intended direction with large sticks or stones, or your backpack or other heavy gear. Move to higher ground, cover your face with a cloth, and wait until the sky clears, keeping your intended direction of travel in mind relative to your position.

FINDING WATER IN THE DESERT

* Dig at the base of cliffs and rock outcroppings.

* Dig beneath the outside edge of a dry streambed.

* Dig in the hollow behind the first sand dune in a coastal desert.

* Follow mosquitoes and especially bees, which are known to fly in a straight line toward water from half a mile away.

* Flip over desert rocks just before dawn—their cool undersides will cause dew to form on the surface at sunrise.

* Soak up dew drops from desert grasses with a piece of cloth, then wring it out over a container.

Out and About

Honeypot ants, native to the desert regions of Australia and North America, have a survival strategy that can also serve as a sugary energy-booster for humans. During rainy spells, worker ants collect water and nectar and force-feed some of their brethren so their abdomens balloon to many times their original size. The colony then stows the engorged, immobile ants in underground chambers, forcing them to regurgitate when food is scarce. In the desert plains of Australia, the black-colored ants live near Mulga trees so they can harvest the nectar of the trees' flowers. To find their hidden treasure, follow an ant to its hole, which will be at ground level unmarked by a mound or protective cover. Use a sharp stick to dig as deep as six feet down into the ants' burrow, where you will find the nectar-yielding ants hanging from the top of the main chamber at the bottom of the shaft. Pick up the swollen ants and squeeze their abdomens to release their honey onto your tongue, or eat them whole.

LAND AREA OF THE SAHARA DESERT VS. LAND AREA OF CONTINENTAL UNITED STATES

 =

Area of Sahara Desert	3,320,000 m²
Area of contiguous United States plus Alaska	3,537,438 m²

Which is Worse?

	Santa Ana Winds	Harmattan Winds
Also Known as	"Devil's Breath"	"The Doctor"
Origin	Great Basin in Nevada and Utah	Eastern Sahara Desert
Area Affected	Southwestern California	Northwestern Africa
Season	October through March; peak in December	December through February
Caused by	Cold air trapped in Great Basin has higher pressure than the air near the coast, creating an air vacuum	Trade wind strengthened by low-pressure area over the Gulf of Guinea
Wind Direction	West/southwest	West/southwest
Distributes	Positive ions, dry air, dust from Great Basin Desert	Red, iron-rich Saharan dust; dry, cool air
Blamed for	Spreading forest and brush fires; increasing murder and suicide rates; prompting bad behavior in school children; causing depression	Causing red haze above Canary Islands; loss of millions of dollars due to flight delays and cancellations; spread of meningitis; causing irritable mood of West Africans

WORLD'S LARGEST DESERTS

	Location	Size	Reason to Avoid
Sahara	Africa	3,320,000 m^2	World-record high temperature: 136°F (1922)
Arabian	Middle East	900,000 m^2	Has added danger of quicksand
Gobi	China	500,000 m^2	Winter temperatures below -40°F
Patagonia	Argentina	260,000 m^2	Constant wind in summer; average winter temperature 35°F
Rub'al Khali	Middle East	250,000 m^2	Even Bedouins avoid the Empty Quarter
Great Victoria	Australia	250,000 m^2	Only lakes consist of salt water
Kalahari	Africa	225,000 m^2	Leopards, hyenas, lions
Great Basin	United States	190,000 m^2	Rattlesnakes
Chihuahua	Mexico	175,000 m^2	High altitude intensifies sun
Thar	India/Pakistan	175,000 m^2	India's nuclear testing grounds

TAKLIMAKAN DESERT
"Place of No Return"

BEST KNOWN FOR: Hurricane-force dust storms that can be seen from space

LOCATION: 105,000 square miles in Western China, with the Tian Shan mountains forming the northern border, the Kunlun mountains to the south, and the Pamir mountains to the west

DANGERS: Spring dust storms that can extend as high as 13,000 feet • No vegetation to provide cover in interior desert • Composed entirely of sand • No wildlife, no plantlife, completely desolate in its wasteland interior

LITTLE-KNOWN FACT: 3,000-year-old mummies with European characteristics buried at its edges, along the former route of the ancient Silk Road

Highest point: 4,900 ft • Lowest point: 2,600 ft • Average summer temperature: 77°F • Record high temperature: 100°F • Average winter temperature: 15°F • Record low temperature: -26°F • Highest ground temperature: 167°F • Maximum sand thickness: 1,000 ft • Average rainfall: 1.5 inches per year • Safest way to travel: with camels saddled with blocks of ice for water

HOW TO BUILD AN UNDERGROUND SAND SHELTER

1   Choose a location.
A natural depression or the hollow between two dunes offers the best protection from the wind and weather if a sandstorm erupts.

2   Dig.
Use a shovel, a pot, an empty cup, or your hands to excavate enough sand to form a two- to three-feet-deep trench that is long and wide enough to accommodate your body. Pile the sand around the perimeter of the trench on three sides, leaving open the narrow end downwind of the prevailing breeze.

3   Build the roof.
Spread a tarp or a large swath of fabric over the ground, aligning one side of the tarp with the long end of the trench and anchoring it in place with rocks and sand along one side. Fold the remaining half of the tarp over the pile of sand and rocks and stretch it back over the trench, creating a foot-wide airspace between the two layers. This will create an insulating layer that will keep the trench as cool as possible. Pile more rocks or sand around the edges to anchor the top layer.

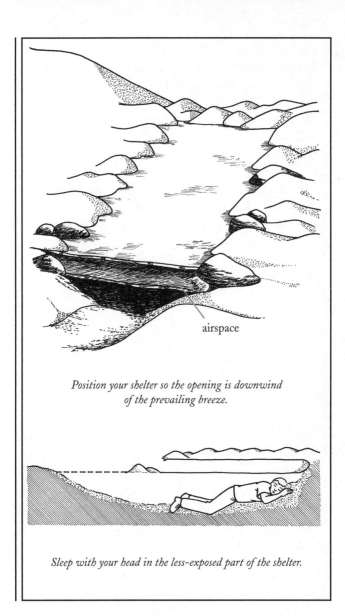

airspace

*Position your shelter so the opening is downwind
of the prevailing breeze.*

Sleep with your head in the less-exposed part of the shelter.

4 Cover the shelter with a reflective or light-colored fabric. Spread a white or reflective fabric over the shelter, creating another airspace between it and the layer of tarp below it. This will block sunlight and may also attract the attention of rescue aircraft.

Be Aware

An underground shelter can reduce heat significantly, but the effort required to build one can hasten dehydration due to sweating. Work when the sun is just rising or just setting, when the air is cooler but there is still enough light to work by.

ESTIMATED SURVIVAL TIME IN THE DESERT WITH LIMITED WATER

RESTING IN THE SHADE

Temperature	No Water	3 Liters	8 Liters
122°F	2–5 days	3–5 days	3–5 days
86°F	5 days	5–8 days	14 days
68°F	12 days	14 days	23–25 days

RESTING BY DAY, WALKING AT NIGHT

Temperature	No Water	3 Liters	8 Liters
122°F	1 day	2 days	3–5 days
86°F	4 days	5 days	5–7 days
68°F	9 days	10–15 days	10–15 days

Out and About

The desert-dwelling horned lizard, commonly referred to as the horny toad, employs a gruesome defense mechanism when captured by a predator. The 3- to 5-inch-long reptile directs a stream of blood from its eyes to deter attack. The blood is produced in the lizard's tear ducts and infused with a chemical that canine predators, such as coyotes and foxes, find offensive. The lizard aims the stream at the canine's mouth, then escapes as the animal tries to wipe or shake the taste from its tongue and teeth.

INTO THE WOODS

Bear Necessities

* **Minimize encounters.** When hiking through known bear territory, make your presence known by wearing a bell, blowing on a whistle, or shouting regularly. When camping, suspend your food in a bag hung over a tree branch far from where you are sleeping.

* **If you see a bear at a distance, stop moving in the bear's direction.** Slowly retreat in the direction you came from until the bear is out of sight. Wait for at least 20 minutes before progressing again, and then move forward with caution, while making noise to alert the bear to your presence.

* **If you see a bear at close range, stand still and be quiet.** Show no fear, but do not make eye contact with the bear. If you have a canister of pepper spray, prepare to use it. If the bear does not take aggressive action, slowly back away while facing the bear and speaking in a low monotone. Do not turn your back to the bear.

* **If the bear charges you, stand your ground.** Many bear charges are bluffs that can turn into an attack if you react with fear, scream, or run away. If the charge stops short of you, remain still and quiet, then slowly back away while facing the bear, speaking in a low monotone.

* **If the bear follows through on the attack, direct a stream of pepper spray into its face.** If that does not deter the bear, or if you do not have pepper spray, play dead—though if the bear continues to maul you, fight back aggressively with whatever tools you have at your disposal.

WOODSMAN ATTACKED BY GRIZZLY, CRAWLS 200 MILES FOR HELP

Fur trapper and frontiersman Hugh Glass was traveling through the area near South Dakota's Grand River in 1823 when he stumbled upon a grizzly bear with two cubs. Attacked by the mother bear before he could fire his rifle, Glass wrestled the bear as it mauled him repeatedly with its claws. Two of his traveling companions responded to his cries for help and shot the animal in the head, but the bear collapsed atop a severely wounded Glass, crushing him. Persuaded that the unconscious Glass would never survive his injuries, the expedition party continued on, leaving two men behind to give him a proper burial when he died. According to the men's report, an Indian attack forced them to give up their death watch after several days. They placed the unconscious Glass in the grave they'd dug, covered him with a bearskin, and left him to die alone, taking his knife, gun, and supplies with them. But Glass woke up. He had a broken leg and deep cuts exposing several of his ribs, and Fort Kiowa, the nearest settlement, was more than 200 miles away. He made a splint for his broken leg and staved off gangrene by letting maggots into his wounds to eat away the dead flesh. Subsisting primarily on roots and berries, drifting in and out of consciousness, Glass crawled through the wilderness for two months until he reached the Cheyenne River. From there he dragged himself to Fort Kiowa, where he recovered his strength.

Expert Advice: Most bear attacks result from surprise encounters, so make plenty of noise while walking through bear country, to ward off attacks before they occur.

Escaping from Forest Animals

Animal	Strategy	When Attacked
Bear	Back away slowly	Stand your ground, use pepper spray, or play dead
Snake	Back away slowly	Wash bite area with soap and water as soon as possible; keep the bite lower than your heart
Mountain Lion	Use your arms and clothing to make yourself look as big as possible; back away slowly	Fight back, striking the animal's eyes and mouth
Wolf	Back away slowly toward firm ground	Charge one member of the pack, shouting and throwing rocks and sticks
Gorilla	Behave submissively; pet and groom the gorilla if it is close to you	Curl up into a ball to protect yourself; remain submissive
Killer Bees	Run away without swatting at the bees	Remove stinger by raking fingernail across stinger in a sideways motion; do not push more venom into your body by squeezing the stinger
Fire Ants	Brush ants from your body as you flee the area	Treat bites with antihistamine; if pustules form, treat with a solution of half water, half bleach

HOW TO SURVIVE AN ENCOUNTER WITH A BIGFOOT

1 Avert your gaze.

A bigfoot may interpret direct eye contact as an attempt at domination and may react unpredictably. Keep it in your peripheral vision to monitor its actions.

2 Remain quiet.

A bigfoot will probably maintain its distance unless it feels you are attempting to annex its territory. Do not shout or open your arms to appear larger, as it may read your actions as a challenge.

3 Control your dog.

Bigfoots may attack aggressive dogs that chase or threaten them.

4 Behave like a forest animal.

To appear less threatening, sit down and scratch yourself as an animal might. Eat, or pretend to eat, anything within reach. If you are with a companion, "groom" him by focusing on pieces of leaves or dirt on his body and picking them off with your hands.

5 Do not attempt to outrun a bigfoot.
Bigfoots may be able to run at speeds of up to 40 miles per hour, as fast as a typical horse.

6 Do not attempt to outswim a bigfoot.
Bigfoots are likely powerful swimmers, both above and below the water.

7 Do not attempt to hide from a bigfoot.
Bigfoots are thought to have a keen sense of smell and excellent night vision.

8 Shine a flashlight in its face.
Bigfoots may be bothered by bright lights and will likely retreat if they are caught in a spotlight.

Be Aware

- There have been roughly 2,000 to 6,000 Bigfoot sightings in North America. They have been spotted in remote wooded, mountainous, or swampy areas as far north as Alaska and the Yukon to as far south as New Mexico and Texas. They are most often reported in the forests of Washington, Oregon, and Northern California.
- Bigfoot sightings generally describe a creature roughly eight feet tall and weighing 650 to 1,000 pounds. At that size, they would likely be able to throw rocks and barrels that weigh as much as 450 pounds, and be capable of lifting cars and trailers off the ground.

Bigfoots are most active at night.

COMMON EDIBLE FOREST PLANTS

Species	Characteristics	Habitat	Edible Parts	How to Eat
Pawpaw	Short, pyramid-shaped trees; alternating leaves; oblong fruits 3 to 5 inches long	Moist soil; river valleys, streambeds	Green or brown fruits are ripe when soft	Raw
Oak Acorn	Round with beret-like cap	Temperate forests	Nuts	Soak in water for 2 days or more; boil or pound into flour
Day Lily	Swordlike leaves and unspotted blossoms	Tropical and temperate forests	Tuber roots	Boil
Nettle	Leaves and stems covered with thin, stinging bristles; tiny flowers	Moist soil; streambeds	Young shoots and leaves	Boil for 15 minutes to destroy bristles
Pokeweed	3-foot-long elliptical leaves; clusters of purple berries	Forest clearings	Leaves, berries	Boil in two changes of water
Chestnut	Tall trunks; broad leaves with widely spaced teeth; ripe nuts are dark	Meadow edges	Nuts	Bake in embers or boil in water

//

EATING LIZARDS

Virtually all lizards are edible, but some have glands that contain toxins.
Before cooking a lizard, cut it from shoulder to shoulder and discard the
head and neck, where poisonous glands are located.

//

Universal Edibility Test

1. Abstain from eating for 8 hours before testing a new possible
   food source.

2. Separate the plant into its basic components: seeds, leaves,
   stems, flowers, buds, and roots.

3. Test for contact poisoning by placing the plant part in the crook
   of your elbow for 15 minutes. If no irritation follows, proceed.

4. Place the plant part on your lips for 3 minutes to make sure it
   won't cause a burning or itching sensation.

5. Place the plant part on your tongue for 15 minutes to make sure
   it causes no irritation.

6. If there has been no adverse reaction, chew a small portion and
   hold it in your mouth for 15 minutes.

7. If no irritation or numbness results, swallow the small plant
   morsel.

8. Abstain from eating anything else for 8 hours. If vomiting or
   nausea ensues, drink plenty of water to flush out your system. If
   there are no adverse effects, prepare a small handful of the plant
   part and eat the whole portion. If another 8 hours pass without
   irritation or vomiting, consider the plant safe to eat.

HOW TO BUILD A WARM BED ON A COLD FOREST FLOOR

1 Clear a rectangular area that is long and wide enough to lie down in.

Brush away dead leaves and pine needles, scraping into the dirt if necessary. If possible, select a spot that is already sheltered on one side by trees or boulders.

2 Spread an even layer of rocks over the bed area.

3 Build a fire over the rocks.

Let the fire burn down, then spread the embers evenly over the hot rocks.

4 Cover the rocks and coals with at least six inches of dirt.

The underlying heat will continue to rise, keeping you warm into the night.

5 Arrange a series of long logs to create a platform above the dirt mound.

6 Pile leaves, pine needles, and other soft materials on top of the wooden platform.

Fill in the grooves between the logs to make a more even surface to lay on.

7 Dress in layers.

Cover your body with extra clothing, tarps, and any

other insulating material to trap your body heat while you sleep.

Be Aware

Sleeping directly on a cold forest floor can conduct heat away from your body, especially in wet conditions. A makeshift bed will insulate you from the icy earth.

Cover the hot rocks with dirt.

Layer pine needles, leaves, and other soft material on logs to even out the surface.

//

BUILDING A FIRE IN THE SNOW

To make a dry bed for your fire in snow-covered terrain, gather green logs
about as thick as your forearm. Arrange half of them parallel to one another,
forming a square platform, then arrange the other half crosswise across the
lower layer. Use dry wood to build your fire on top of the platform.

//

MYTH: A tick transmits Lyme disease as soon as it attaches
to your body.

FACT: It takes from 24 to 48 hours for the tick to begin transmitting the bacteria that cause Lyme disease. If you remove the tick within this amount of time, before the tick becomes engorged, your chances of getting Lyme disease are low. Inspect your body thoroughly after visiting deer tick territory. Remove any ticks with small tweezers, grasping their bodies as close to the skin as possible. Do not crush the tick's midsection, where the disease resides. Use the tweezers to remove any mouth parts left behind in the wound. Wash the site with antibacterial soap. If subsequent swelling takes the form of a red bull's-eye, see your doctor.

SKIER INJURED, STUCK ALONE IN FOREST WITHOUT SUPPLIES

After a three-mile ski and a light lunch on the trails near Steamboat Springs, Colorado, 55-year-old cross-country skier Charles Horton turned to head back to his van, only to lose his balance as one ski plunged through the surface of the snow. The bone plate beneath his knee shattered, as well as his tibia and two ribs. He was 9,000 feet above sea level, he could barely move, and the only people who knew of his ski plans were out of town. After removing his skis, Horton rolled onto his back and used his elbows to drag himself toward the shelter of a pine tree. As he'd only prepared for a half-day trip, his water was all gone, and he'd eaten all his food for lunch. He cut off low-hanging branches with a pocketknife and lit a fire with the few matches he had in his pocket, then he went to sleep in below-freezing temperatures. As the days passed he willed himself to live, melting snow in his mouth to quench his thirst and slithering down the trail he had skied up, but he collapsed in exhaustion after making it less than a mile from the site of his accident. A week after he'd left on his afternoon jaunt, a blizzard rolled through, covering him with eight inches of snow. He'd all but given up hope when, on the eighth day, he heard a whistle through the woods. He pulled out his own emergency whistle and responded—allowing the search party to pinpoint his location and carry him to safety.

Expert Advice: Most wilderness emergencies occur when an injury turns a day trip into an extended ordeal for which the traveler is not prepared. When trekking alone in the cold, always bring a whistle and an emergency blanket.

BEST FIREWOODS

Species	Heat per Cord (million BTUs)	Smoke	Sparks	Ease of Burning	Ease of Splitting
Apple	26–27	Minimal	Few	Poor	Easy
Oak	24–27	Minimal	Few	Poor	Hard
Beech	24–27	Minimal	Few	Poor	Easy
Birch	20-26	Minimal	Moderate	Good	Easy
Ash	19–24	Minimal	Few	Fair	Easy
Elm	19–20	Some	Few	Fair	Hard
Maple	18–19	Minimal	Few	Good	Hard
Aspen	15	Some	Few	Fair	Easy
Pine	14–15	Some	Moderate	Poor	Easy
Cedar	12–13	Some	Many	Fair	Easy

///

BAD SMOKE

Do not burn poison oak, poison ivy, or wood from or covered in any plants that are known to cause skin irritation. The allergy-spurring oils are most concentrated on the stems, and inhaling them through smoke may provoke respiratory problems.

///

OUTDOORSMAN KEEPS HIS WITS, SURVIVES FRIGID NIGHT

Dick Arsenault was tracking a deer in Maine's White Mountains when the December night closed in around him and he realized he'd gone deeper into the woods than he had intended. Having lost his compass in thick brush earlier in the day, the experienced outdoorsman decided that the best course of action would be to set a fire and wait until daylight. But as the temperature dropped and the spruce branches he gathered produced more smoke than heat, he needed to change tacks. Arsenault knew that his truck was parked to his south, a swamp occupied the territory to his west, and Canada lay to the north and east. The overcast sky prevented him from fixing upon the North Star to get his bearings, but he did know two important pieces of information: most of the airplanes in that vicinity followed flight plans across Canadian airspace, and the prevailing winds were usually from the north. He put his back to the breeze, made sure the sounds of aircraft were coming from behind him, and began walking toward what he hoped would be the logging road where he had left his truck. Despite the lack of a flashlight, Arsenault made steady progress for a number of hours—until he attempted to traverse a frozen bog. The icy surface crumpled and he fell in up to his knees. Arsenault decided there was little chance of drying out his boots since his fire-building efforts had failed him the first time around. He plodded along until morning, when a rescue plane spotted him just as he approached his truck.

Expert Advice: Once you have decided on a plan of escape, stick with it and stay in motion—especially if your body heat is the only thing keeping you warm on a bitter cold night.

HOW TO BUILD A BRIDGE ACROSS A FRIGID RIVER

1 Anchor a short, thick log to the riverbank.
Find or chop a log measuring approximately two feet long and at least one foot thick. Lay it on the ground parallel to the river, about two feet from the water. Drive several stakes into the ground on either side of the log to hold it in place.

2 Find a log for the bridge.
The log should be long enough to span the river with three feet of clearance on either side.

3 Test the weight-bearing capacity of your log.
Lift one end of the long log onto the log you've anchored next to the river; prop the other end of the long log onto a tree stump or a flat stone tall enough to lift the log off the ground. Step on the middle of the span to test its strength. If it doesn't break, it's safe to use.

4 Drag the long log next to the anchor log.
Place the log parallel to the river, between the water and the anchor, so that one end lines up with the end of the anchor.

Wedge the log in the corner formed by the anchor log and the rock.
Pull the log into a vertical position, then lower it across the river.

5 Place a heavy stone next to the anchor at the end of the long log.
Form a solid corner between the stone and the anchor. This will keep the bridge log from sliding as you maneuver it into position.

6 Tie a rope around the far end of the long log.
If you are working alone, leave enough slack in the rope to span the width of the river. If you have help and enough rope, leave twice as much slack.

7 Raise the log to a vertical position.
Using the stone and the anchor to prevent slippage, pull on the rope to stand the long log straight up.

8 Lower the log across the river.
Slowly let out the rope so the far end of the log ends up on the opposite bank.

9 Elevate the bridge if necessary.
If the riverbank is soggy and the log is touching the cold water, prop the near end of the log on the anchor to provide more space between the river and the bridge.

Forest Insects

Species	Range	Weaponry	Pain
Bullet Ants	Atlantic Coast, South and Central America	One of the most powerful insect venoms on earth	Likened to a three-inch nail in the foot
Jack Jumper Ants	Australia, Tasmania	Stings that can trigger allergic reactions, sometimes fatally	Pain, local swelling can last for days
Wheel Bug	United States, especially Florida	8 to 12 teeth can cause a skin wound lasting one year	Burning and numbness
Killer Bees	South and Central America, southern United States	Swarms attack humans with multiple stings, potentially causing death	Localized itching and swelling
Deer Ticks	Northeastern United States	Bites can spread Lyme disease	No pain

CHAMPION TREES

TALLEST

Species	Tallest Specimen	Location
Coast Redwood	378 feet	Redwood National Park, California
Coast Douglas Fir	329 feet	Coos County, Oregon
Australian Mountain Ash	318 feet	Styx Valley, Tasmania
Sitka Spruce	317 feet	Prairie Creek Redwoods State Park, California

OLDEST

Species	Oldest Specimen	Location
Great Basin Bristlecone Pine	4,844 years	White Mountains, California
Alerce Cypress	3,635 years	Chile
Giant Sequoia	3,200 years	Sierra Nevada, California

LARGEST BY VOLUME

Species	Biggest Specimen	Location
Giant Sequoia	1,489 cubic meters	Sierra Nevada, California
Coast Redwood	1,045 cubic meters	Jedidiah Smith Park, California
Kauri	517 cubic meters	Waipoua Forest, New Zealand
Western Redcedar	500 cubic meters	Quinault Lake, Washington

WEIGHT OF GIANT SEQUOIA VS. EARTH'S LARGEST ANIMALS

=

 x 10

Blue Whale
about 140 tons

=

 x 275

Elephant
about 5 tons

**General Sherman,
the giant sequoia
in California's
Sierra Nevada**
1,385 tons

HOW TO BUILD A WIGWAM

Whether you are seeking protection from the elements or wild animals, a wigwam provides a robust shelter that has the added benefit of natural camouflage.

1 Draw a circle in the dirt in a flat, dry place.
Use a stick about as tall as you are to measure the radius of the circle your wigwam will be built upon, drawing sixteen evenly spaced hash marks in the dirt around the ring.

2 Dig holes for the support poles.
At each mark, use a blunt rock to pound a sharpened stake into the ground, making a narrow hole at least 6 inches deep.

3 Collect 30 saplings for the frame.
Choose flexible saplings 10 to 12 feet long and between 1 and 2 inches thick. Strip the outer layer of bark on each sapling with a pocket knife.

4 Build the main frame.
Envision the circle as a clock dial. Drive two saplings securely into the pair of holes on either side of the 12 o'clock position. Do the same at 3, 6, and 9 o'clock sites. Bend each sapling across the interior of the circle to meet the one directly across from it, lashing the ends together with duct tape or twine. The resulting

*Cover the dome with bark peeled from
tree trunks to block the wind.*

domed lattice will resemble a tic-tac-toe board when viewed from above.

5 Build the secondary frame.
Fill the remaining holes with eight more of the prepared saplings. Bend each one across the circle and bind it to its counterpart.

6 Fortify the structure with hoops.
Lash the remaining saplings to one another to make four successively smaller hoops around the outside of the structure. Starting with the biggest hoop closest to the ground, secure each hoop to the domed frame using duct tape or twine.

7 Cover the dome with canvas, bark sheets, or mats woven from long grasses.
Bark sheets can be peeled from the trunks of elm, hickory, ash, and chestnut trees. Leave space at one side of the dome for a door.

8 Add a few more poles to keep the covering materials in place.
Bend more saplings and place them as in steps 5 and 6.

LEWIS AND CLARK ESCAPE STARVATION IN THE BITTERROOTS

After a difficult crossing of the Continental Divide, Meriwether Lewis and William Clark embarked on the most treacherous part of their cross-country expedition. As August gave way to a cold September in 1805, the explorers led a party of about 30 men and 27 horses into the heavily forested Bitterroot Mountains of Montana and Idaho. Negotiating terrain "as steep as the roof of a house," as one man wrote, the group was unable to find game for their hunters. They finished the last of their pork provisions on September 3, leaving only dried corn, thin emergency soup, and some bear oil. The steep slopes caused their horses to fall, and frigid swamps clotted with beaver dams frustrated their progress. As the men pressed on, temperatures dropped so low their moccasins froze on their feet. On September 14, after a week in which the hunters had only been able to kill a single deer and some small pheasants to feed all 30 men and their animals, the men were forced to kill one of their colts for food. Rain turned to hail, then to snow. Three days later, they had to kill and eat another horse. Scouts spotted a valley ahead, but it proved to be twice as far away as their estimate. The men killed a third horse. Finally, on September 22, Lewis and Clark made it over the range and encountered the Nez Perce Indians, who provided them with salmon and edible roots, rescuing the men from the brink of starvation and allowing them to continue with their expedition.

Expert Advice: When traveling in a big group, always scout unknown territory before traversing it—paying special attention to how much food you can expect to find on your journey.

TOTAL FOREST COVER BY CONTINENT*

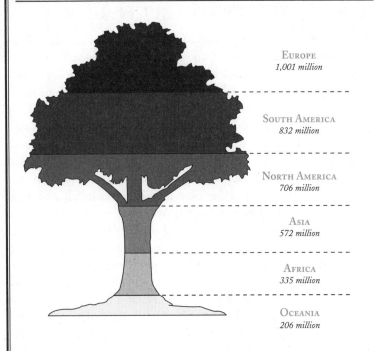

EUROPE
1,001 million

SOUTH AMERICA
832 million

NORTH AMERICA
706 million

ASIA
572 million

AFRICA
335 million

OCEANIA
206 million

Total: 3,952 million hectares, or about 30 percent of land on Earth

*Measured in hectares.

Highest Annual Deforestation Rate*

Nigeria
82,000

Sudan
117,800

Bolivia
215,200

U.S.
224,600

Peru
224,600

Papua New Guinea
250,200

Mexico
395,000

Indonesia
532,200

Russia
1,447,800

Brazil
3,466,000

*Measured in hectares.

Rule of Thumb for Edible Berries

Characteristic	Chance It's Safe to Eat
White	10 percent
Yellow	10 percent
Red	50 percent
Blue	90 percent
Black	90 percent

//

THE ANTI-ITCH PLANT

Between bee stings, ant bites, and poison plants—usually ivy, oak, or sumac—the forest abounds with potential for itches and rashes. If you're not carrying steroid cream or calamine lotion, use jewelweed as a natural balm to reduce skin irritation. Common in streambeds and sunny stretches of moist earth, jewelweed can be identified by its trumpet-shaped orange or yellow flowers, and seedpods that audibly pop when touched. To tap its anti-itching properties, crush a handful of leaves and stems into a tight wad, and vigorously rub the plant's juices into the affected area.

//

HOW TO ESCAPE A FOREST FIRE

1 Monitor the horizons.

If you see smoke rising above the trees in the distance, watch to see if it increases in size or strength. If so, move upwind and down-slope, away from the fire.

2 Watch for burning embers.

The wind may blow embers more than half a mile from their origin; remain alert to avoid getting burned, and be ready to change course in case a stray ember ignites another area of the forest.

3 Find a firebreak.

Move to a pond, river, road, rocky area, open field, or another area lacking in burnable fuel. Avoid areas thick with brush and dried grasses, as these materials burn fast and hot. Do not climb uphill, as the fire and superheated air will updraft on even the slightest slope, concentrating the flames and heat most intensely in these chimneys.

4 Seek a gap in the fire line.

A forest fire may advance across a front several miles wide, but it does not always travel at a uniform rate. If you are trapped by a wall of fire, look for a spot where the flames are thin and low to the ground. If possible, cloak your body in natural fibers (synthetic materials may melt and burn your skin) and soak yourself with water. Wrap a wet cloth around your mouth and nose.

Cover your face and head with your arms and run through a thin line of fire as fast as possible. If the moisture in the cloth around your mouth turns into steam, take it off to protect your lungs.

5 If you are trapped on a hillside, move to an outward curve in the trail.

The contour of the land can concentrate intensely hot air currents in protected pockets and indentations on the hillside. The outward rounding bends on the outside of a hill provide a safer location; the heat is more diffuse and travels more slowly. Position yourself as far away from the trail's outer edge as possible to avoid rising heat. Once the fire has burned up the chimneys, you may be able to move to the burnt area before the fire reaches the outside curve.

6 Crawl in a ditch.

If the fire is near and you cannot find another means of escape, lie down in a ditch with your feet facing the direction of the fire. Cover your feet, legs, and body with as much dirt and noncombustible material as possible. Wait for the fire to pass completely before getting back up.

7 Signal passing aircraft to seek their attention.

Wave white or brightly colored clothing or shine a reflective mirror toward the airplane. If the plane contains fire personnel, they will likely provide you with instructions over their loudspeaker.

*Run to already-burned areas, clearings, water,
or an outward curve in the trail.*

Be Aware

- A field of grass can produce a fire more than 10 feet tall that moves at a rate of 20 mph. Deciduous trees burn more slowly than grass but can elevate temperatures to preheat the nearby trees, causing them to ignite more quickly. The needles and resin in pine trees are highly combustible and will rapidly spread a very hot fire.

- Dangerous wild animals, such as rattlesnakes, bears, and mountain lions, will also be anxious to escape the fire and may cross your path as you seek safety.

- If you are surrounded by a forest fire while you're in your vehicle, remain inside the vehicle rather than attempting escape on foot—the protection offered by the car outweighs the relatively low risk that your gas tank will explode in the heat. Drive to low, bare ground as free from brush and trees as possible and park facing the oncoming fire. Roll up the windows, shut all air vents, and turn on your hazards and headlights to make the car more visible to rescuers. Lie on the floor below window-level and cover your head and face with blankets to protect yourself from radiant heat. Smoke will enter the vehicle as the fire surrounds the car, so take shallow breaths close to the floor, breathing through a damp cloth. Stay in the vehicle until fire passes and the radiant heat has dissipated enough that the air feels no hotter than the heat felt from a bad sunburn. The door handles and interior car parts will be extremely hot; do not touch them with bare skin.

Worst Forest Fires in North American History

Name	Date	Location	Acres Burned	Casualties
Miramichi	October 1825	Maine and New Brunswick, Canada	3,000,000	160 people
Peshtigo	October 1871	Wisconsin and Michigan	3,378,000	1,500 people
Lower Michigan	September 1881	Michigan	2,500,000	169 people
Great Idaho	August 1910	Idaho and Montana	3,000,000	85 people
Cloquet–Moose Lake	October 1918	Minnesota	1,200,000	450 people
Yellowstone	July–August 1988	Montana and Idaho	1,585,000	No human casualties
Mexico's El Niño Fires	May–June 1998	Mexico	1,250,000	23+ people
Okanagan Mountain Park	August 2003	British Columbia	60,000	No human casualties
Southern California	October 2003	Southern California	800,000	22 people
Taylor Complex	August 2004	Alaska	1,305,000	No human casualties

UNPREPARED REPORTER LOSES MORE THAN A STORY IN THE AMAZON

Journalist Joe Kane's trip to the Ecuadorian Amazon for a report on the Huaorani Indians didn't work out the way he'd planned. First, the Huaorani, a hunter-gatherer people known for killing outsiders, ate Kane's three-week supply of food in four days. Then, soon after Kane and his interpreter set out on their planned journey across the rainforest, their local guide abandoned them after seeing a giant snake he considered a bad omen, leaving the unprepared walkers in the care of a 12-year-old and two inexperienced teenagers. Several days of walking over difficult terrain shattered both of Kane's big toenails, making each step more painful than the last. And though he was carrying a shotgun, he was unable to hunt for food, having already traded away his shotgun shells. After Kane and his compatriots ate the last morsels of their emergency food supply, the group boiled a small turtle they found on the trail, their only meal for the next two days. Then, despite reaching the general section of the forest they'd been aiming for, the group got lost. Kane asked his interpreter what that meant for their chances. "It means we might die," the man said. Kane already felt himself slowly starving to death. Upon reaching a river they could not identify, Kane's young companions lashed together two rafts from tree trunks and vines and made paddles from saplings. They floated down the river for a full day, water up to their hips, without any improvement in their circumstances. But finally their luck turned—on their second day on the river, they encountered a motored canoe piloted by a friend of Kane's interpreter, filled with two dead monkeys, turkey carcasses, and bananas.

Expert Advice: Never venture into the rainforest without weapons suitable for hunting game.

MYTH: Moss only grows on the north side of trees.

FACT: Although moss favors shaded surfaces, which in the northern hemisphere are likely to be surfaces that face north, navigating through the woods based on the location of moss is a sure way to get lost. A dense forest scatters and blocks most direct sunlight, including the predominant southern light that might discourage moss from growing on a sun-exposed tree. If a forest is thick enough to make getting lost a concern, it is probably thick enough to allow moss to grow wherever it takes root.

Out and About

The Asian silver carp, a species native to China's Yangtze River but imported to the United States in the 1980s, poses an unusual threat to fishermen and river travelers. When the fish are startled by the sound of a boat motor or any other unusual noise, they home in on the source and jump as high as eight feet out of the water. Weighing as much as 20 pounds, the airborne carp routinely strike boaters with blows that have been likened to collisions with slimy bowling balls. When the fish leap in schools, the volleys can be enough to knock adults off their feet. Since they breed faster than native species in the United States and are fierce competitors for food, Asian silver carp have infiltrated 15 states along the Mississippi and Missouri rivers. The best way to avoid or escape attack is to turn off the boat motor and move away quietly.

HOW TO MAKE A BUNDLE BOW AND ARROWS

1 Collect the sticks for your bow.

Find three sticks of uniform thickness, each between two and four feet long and preferably of a lightweight, sturdy wood like bamboo, pine, ash, willow, or elm. Consider your arm strength when choosing sticks—thicker sticks provide more resistance as you pull back the bowstring, but a thicker bow also leads to faster-flying arrows.

2 Cut the sticks to size.

Cleanly sever the ends of the sticks to make each one a different length. One stick should measure between three and four feet, another should be half as long, and the last should be three-quarters the size of the longest stick.

3 Bind the sticks together.

Lay the shortest stick next to the longest one, centering it so there is equal empty space on either side of the longer stick. Secure the two sticks together using strong adhesive tape or rope. Bind the medium-sized stick to the other two, centering it on top of the other two to produce a bow that is thickest in the middle and tapers out toward the ends. Use a pocket knife to carve a notch about an inch from the tip on either side of the longest stick.

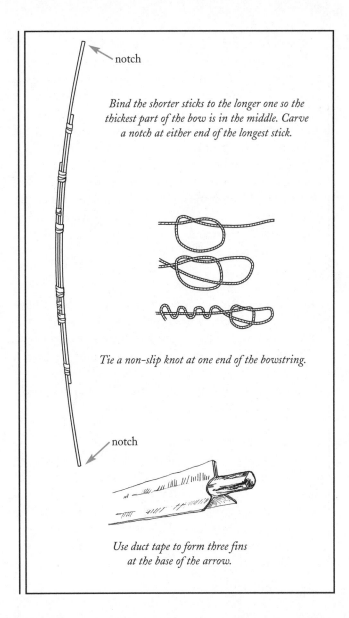

notch

Bind the shorter sticks to the longer one so the thickest part of the bow is in the middle. Carve a notch at either end of the longest stick.

Tie a non-slip knot at one end of the bowstring.

notch

Use duct tape to form three fins at the base of the arrow.

4 Make a bowstring.

Select a single strong cord about as long as the bow, or braid together several lengths of strong twine, to make a bowstring that will not stretch or break when it's secured to the bow. To test the string's strength, stand on one end, hold the other in one hand, and pull; if the string stretches, braid in another strand of cord. Tie a non-slip loop knot at one end of the string. (Begin by tying a loose overhand knot six inches from the end of the string. Thread the end back through the center of the knot, creating a loop, and wrap it around the other side of the string four times. Pass the end back through the center of the knot.)

5 Attach the string to the bow.

Drape the loop in the knot over the top end of the bow, letting it slip beneath the notch you have cut. Tie the other end of the string securely to the notch at the bottom end of the bow, using the standard knot you prefer. Bending the bow, slip the looped end of the string up the shaft of the bow until it settles in the upper notch. The bow should now be moderately flexed.

6 Gather wooden shoots for your arrows.

Locate and harvest straight branches about two inches longer than the distance from the bow to the back of the bowstring when the bow is flexed. Dry them in a shelter or cave or by suspending them from a tree branch in arid weather. (This may take several days, depending on the weather.) Whittle one end of each shoot to a sharp point.

7 | Attach fletching to the arrow base.

Cut three lengths of sturdy adhesive tape about six inches long. Bend one piece of tape lengthwise so it forms the shape of a U, with the sticky side facing outward. Stick the curve of the U onto the arrow, running parallel to the shaft; each side of the U should stick up in the air. Bend the second piece of tape in the same manner, sticking it to the arrow about one-third of the distance from the first piece of tape. Fold the last length of tape in the same manner, putting it midway between the first two pieces. Ensure that the tape completely encases the shaft, then press each tape flap against the flap beside it, forming three fins. To stabilize the arrow in flight, trim the fins so they are thickest at the back end of the shaft, tapering down to nothing toward the pointed front end.

IT'S A JUNGLE
OUT THERE

TROPICAL DISEASES

Disease	Spread by	Geographical Range	Symptoms	Fatality Rate	Treatment
Yellow Fever	Mosquitoes	Africa, South America	Fever, headache, vomiting, muscle aches	15–50%	No specific treatment; quarantine, rest and fluids recommended
Dengue Fever	Mosquitoes	Africa, Asia, Americas, Pacific, Caribbean	Fever, rash, pain behind the eyes, headache, nausea, vomiting, loss of appetite	2–5%	No specific treatment; quarantine, rests, and fluids recommended; blood transfusion may be required
Malaria	Anopheles mosquitoes	Asia, Africa, Central and South America	Fever, chills, flu-like symptoms	15–30%	Prescription drugs
Japanese Encephalitis	Mosquitoes	Asia	Fever, chills, tiredness, headache, nausea, vomiting (or no symptoms at all)	30–60%	No specific treatment
Meningococcal Disease	Person-to-person contact (respiratory droplets)	Central Africa	Fever, headache, nausea, vomiting, rash, stiff neck	10–50%	Antibiotics
Amoebic Dysentery	Contaminated food and water	All tropical settings	Bloody diarrhea, stomach cramps	5%	Antibiotics

JAPANESE STRAGGLER FOUND ON GUAM 27 YEARS AFTER END OF WORLD WAR II

Sergeant Shoichi Yokoi survived in the jungles of Guam for 27 years after World War II was officially over and his family had given him up for dead. Yokoi was a soldier in the Japanese army; most of his unit was killed or escaped after the Americans invaded the island in July 1944, but in the confusion of battle, Yokoi headed into the mountains and was cut off from his compatriots. Though he'd discovered a pamphlet in 1952 that revealed that the war was over, Yokoi chose to live off the land rather than turn himself in, and he used every resource imaginable to survive. For shelter, he fashioned a trowel from an old cannon shell and dug out a well-hidden cave. He used a lens to start fires and kept an ember constantly burning on a rope of coconut fiber. He also made his own clothes—he beat the bark of a pago tree into fiber, from which he wove cloth; he beat pieces of brass into needles so he could sew the cloth into shirts and pants; he used the plastic from a flashlight to make buttons; he made a belt from woven pago fibers; and he made a belt buckle from wire. Yokoi also crafted tools out of found materials—he cut a canteen in half to make a frying pan and a plate, and he used large pieces of hollowed-out bamboo to collect rainwater and to scoop water from the river. For food, Yokoi picked mangoes, coconuts, and various nuts. He built traps and caught eels, shrimp, and crabs in the river, and he grew fond of roasted rat meat. When he was discovered by two fishermen in 1972, he charged them and tried to fight rather than surrender even then. They eventually captured him and turned him over to the authorities. He returned to Japan and lectured on the topic of survival until his death in 1997.

Expert Advice: Think creatively about the materials you have at hand—use every tool to its full potential.

TROPICAL DRINKS

* **Harvest rainwater from stands of upright bamboo.** Bend a tall stalk of green bamboo toward you, tie it down, and cut off the leaves from the top to create a spigot. Place a container under the hollow bent tube to catch the water, which will drip for several hours.

* **Cut a banana or plantain tree about one foot from the ground and dig a bowl-shaped impression in its stump.** It will immediately begin to fill with water from the roots. The water may be bitter at first, but after the first couple of bowls full it will be tasteless. The bowl will continue to fill for several days.

* **Collect water from pitcher plants.** Large plants can trap up to two liters of rain. (This water frequently harbors insects and occasionally bigger fauna, so purify or filter it before drinking, to avoid disease.)

* **Puncture green coconuts.** Use a knife or machete and drink the liquid inside.

* **Drink from vines.** Cut a deep notch in a vine at the highest point you can reach, then sever it completely as far below the notch as you can. Let the water drip into your mouth, or capture it in a container. If the liquid is milky or white, do not drink it.

HOW TO MAKE A FIRE WITH A SINGLE STALK OF BAMBOO

1 Split a piece of dry bamboo down the middle.
A dry bamboo stalk will be brown or tan and may have brown leaves near the top. Use a machete or sharp stone to crack it down the center. The grain of the bamboo makes it easy to split.

2 Anchor one piece of the bamboo to the ground.
Lay half the split bamboo horizontally on the ground, with the hollow side facing up. Use several wooden stakes to secure it in place.

3 Make a notch halfway down the other piece of bamboo.
Use a pocketknife to make a wedge-shaped notch that is about an inch wide on the outside of the bamboo and a narrow slit on the inside.

4 Gather several sticks of various sizes.
You will use these to feed the fire once it's started.

5 Shave thin filaments from the notched piece of bamboo.
Scrape your machete or a sharp stone back and forth over the split edges. The fine grain will peel off, forming a soft tuft of dry tinder.

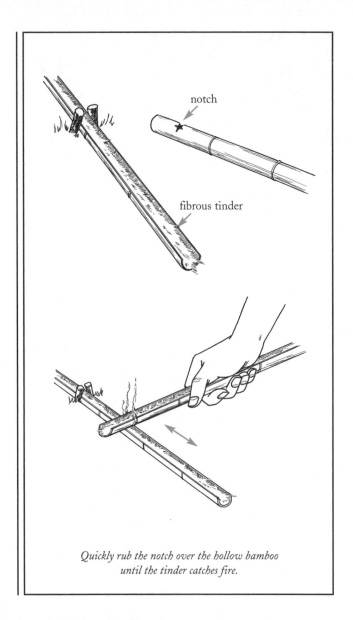

notch

fibrous tinder

*Quickly rub the notch over the hollow bamboo
until the tinder catches fire.*

6 Place the clump of tinder inside the carved notch.
Settle the wide part of the notch on the edges of the anchored bamboo, forming an X. Rapidly drag the top piece of bamboo back and forth to create friction against the anchored stalk. After a while, the tinder will begin to smoke and burn.

7 Nurse the small flame into a full-blown fire.
Place several small, dry sticks on top of the burning tinder, gradually adding larger pieces of fuel until the fire is of the desired size.

Out and About

In recent years, uncontrolled logging and global warming have led to an unexpected consequence in the tropical forests of Borneo—an increase in the number of unprovoked Malaysian sun bear attacks. Though sun bears are the smallest members of the bear family, weighing in at 60 to 150 pounds, they have strong paws with long, sickle-shaped claws and sharp canine teeth they use more to wage battle than to tear into food. Since 2000, the bears have become increasingly aggressive, and they have even pounced unprovoked from the shadows to attack hapless people. The bears' aggression is related to their shrinking habitat. Borneo's rainforest has experienced intense logging since the 1980s; even protected areas, such as Indonesia's Gunung Palung National Park, have been fragmented by illegal, chainsaw-wielding gangs. Additionally, drought and fires caused by the rise in global temperature have hindered the reproduction of the large fruit-bearing trees the ecosystem relies upon for its survival. As the forests shrink, a greater number of bears are concentrated into a smaller space, increasing competition for food and causing the bears to behave more aggressively.

THE BORNEO RAINFOREST

BEST KNOWN FOR: Being one of the oldest tropical jungles on Earth

LOCATION: Indonesian/Malaysian archipelago

DANGERS: Clouded leopards • Largest python species in the world • Bees that home in on human sweat • Tiger leeches • Deadly white-water of the Boh River • Violence between logging interests and native tribes

LITTLE-KNOWN FACT: Before the forest was broken up by palm plantations, the Borneo rainforest canopy was so thick and continuous that orangutans were said to be able to travel from one end of the island to the other without setting foot on the ground.

Highest point: Mount Kinabalu, 13,435 feet • Town most notorious for harboring pirates: Lahad Datu, Malaysia • Most peculiar dietary staple: Sago palm tree trunks, eaten by the Penan nomads • Weirdest funeral custom: Entombing the dead in pottery vases hung from tree branches until the corpses rot • Smelliest flower: Rafflesia, whose scent has been likened to a rotting buffalo carcass

MYTH: It's easy for humans to find food in the rainforest.

FACT: Despite the amazing diversity of plants in each square foot of the jungle, it is difficult for an untrained person to find food. Many low-to-the-ground species are poisonous or covered in protective thorns or spines, and the nonpoisonous species are too high to reach easily. Animals, too, do not provide an abundant food source, as most are located high in the tree canopy.

Out and About

The sago palm tree is a significant food source for the native jungle dwellers of Indonesia, Malaysia, New Guinea, and the Philippines. The mature sago palm is between 30 and 70 feet tall and typically consists of several trunks growing from a single root system. Cutting away the hard outer bark reveals a spongy interior that can be pounded into a granular material. When mixed with water and strained through a cloth, the nutritional components of this granular substance will settle like silt on the bottom of a container. The water is poured off the sediment and the sago is left to dry, becoming a flour that is cooked in a manner similar to oatmeal. A single day of sago flour production can yield five days' worth of sustenance, making it a more efficient means of food procurement than hunting or farming. Sago palms typically grow near rivers or on mountain slopes and ridges, and are especially common at the edges of clearings.

EDIBLE PLANTS IN THE TROPICAL RAINFOREST

Species	Characteristics	Edible Parts	How to Eat
Coconut	Long trunk with thick cluster of large compound leaves at the top	Hard white flesh beneath the hard shell	Liquid: drink; flesh: scrape, sun-dry to preserve
Bamboo	Skinny, segmented green stalks with small green leaves	Young shoots	Raw, or boil to remove bitterness
Banana	Lush, tall plants with large, thick leaves and brown or yellow oblong fruit	Peeled fruit	Raw
Papaya	Small tree with thick crown of leaves and fruit growing straight from the trunk	Peeled fruit	Raw
Mango	Tall tree with long, skinny green leaves and oval-shaped fruit	Peeled fruit	Raw
Yam	Ground-borne vine with heart-shaped leaves	Root tuber	Boil or bake
Taro	Short plants with broad green fronds	Root, leaves, stalk	Boil, changing the water three times before eating
Palm Tree	Long, bare trunk with dense crown of compound leaves	Soft "heart" at the top end of the trunk	Raw, or boil

HOW TO BUILD A JUNGLE SHELTER

1 Clear the vegetation from a flat, dry area.

The space for your shelter need only be slightly longer than your body, and about twice the width. Avoid areas where signs of erosion indicate a danger of flash floods.

2 Drive four posts into the ground, one at each corner of the area.

Collect four logs or branches about as tall as your shoulder and about six inches across. Use a sharpened stick to dig the post holes, then pound a post into each hole to a depth of at least one foot, so the pole stands as tall as your waist.

3 Carve a notch on each pole.

Use a pocketknife or a sharp stick to carve a two-inch notch into the outward face of each pole, at a uniform height just below knee-level.

4 Collect materials for the frame of the structure.

Find six straight sapling trunks or sturdy tree branches about four inches in diameter, or thick enough to hold your weight. You'll need two saplings about 2 feet longer than the width of your shelter area (probably between 5 and 7 feet long) and four more saplings about 2 feet longer than the length of your shelter (between 8 and 10 feet long).

apex

gable

gable

2 feet

Sleep about 2 feet off the ground to protect yourself
from flash floods, insects, fungal infections, hypothermia,
and wild animal attacks.

5 Create the frame at the head and foot of the shelter.
Form a horizontal bar by placing the ends of one of the shorter saplings into the notches in the poles at the head of the shelter. Repeat at the foot of the shelter. Secure both saplings to the poles with rope or vines. Ideally, the ends of both crossbars should protrude about one foot beyond the posts they're resting on.

6 Create the frame for the sides of the shelter.
Use two of the long remaining saplings to form the crossbars for the sides, laying them on top of the protruding ends of the crossbars at the shelter's top and bottom. Lash them in place with ropes or vines.

7 Make a bed from sturdy, smaller branches.
Gather several dozen straight branches about two inches in diameter and about two feet longer than the width of the shelter frame. Place them so that they span from one side of the frame to the other, and lash them in place with ropes or vines.

8 Collect materials to make the roof.
Find five straight branches or saplings measuring about two inches in diameter: one should be two feet longer than the length of the shelter (this will form the apex), and the other four should be two feet longer than the width of the shelter (these will form the gables).

9 Make the frame for the roof.
Carve a two-inch notch into the outward face of each upright pole an inch or two from the top. Lay the two

remaining long and thick saplings gathered in step 4 into the notches to create another pair of lengthwise crossbars at the top of the shelter. Lash a pair of gable branches together at one end, creating a right angle between them; then lash the free ends to the top of the head posts. Repeat with the other gable branches at the foot of the shelter. Finally, lash the long apex sapling into the V shape at the top of each gable, creating a lengthwise crossbar for your roof.

10 Finish the roof.
Fill in the frame by lashing branches that run horizontally from one end of the shelter to the other. These branches should be about an inch thick, or sturdy enough to support heavy leaves. Drape large leaves over the roof frame, overlapping them from top to bottom to form natural shingles.

Be Aware
An elevated shelter is essential in tropical environments. Sleeping directly on the ground may lead to fungal infections; leech infestation; attacks from wild boars, snakes, and other large animals; hypothermia; or drowning by flash flood.

Rainiest Places on Earth

	Location	Rainfall
Highest average annual rainfall, South America	Lloro, Colombia	523 inches
Highest average annual rainfall, Asia	Mawsynram, India	467 inches
Highest average annual rainfall, Pacific	Mount Waialeale, Hawaii	460 inches
Highest average annual rainfall, Africa	Debundscha, Cameroon	405 inches
Most rain in a single year	Cherrapunji, India	905 inches
Most rain in a single day	Baguio, Philippines	46 inches
Most rain in a 5-minute period	Portobelo, Panama	2.5 inches
Wettest city, South America	Buenaventira, Colombia	267 inches per year
Wettest city, Africa	Monrovia, Liberia	202 inches per year
Wettest city, Pacific	Pago Pago, American Samoa	202 inches per year
Wettest city, Asia	Moulmein, Myanmar	192 inches per year

CRASH SURVIVOR NAVIGATES RAINFOREST WITH BROKEN COLLARBONE

On Christmas Eve, 1971, lightning struck the plane carrying 17-year-old Juliane Koepcke over the Peruvian rainforest. The row of three seats that Koepcke was buckled into was thrown into the air, and she fell headfirst for several thousand feet until she crashed through the jungle canopy and struck the soil below. Koepcke awoke to discover that she had a small open wound on her arm, a broken collarbone, and one eye too swollen to see out of. Dressed in a miniskirt, blouse, and one sandal, she pulled herself upright and looked for other crash survivors, but she was alone. For several days she caught glimpses of search planes, but she was unable to get their attention. Then they stopped coming. Despite her broken collarbone, Koepcke began walking. She found a small spring and followed the water to a bigger creek; having grown up in the rainforest, she reasoned that it would lead to a river, and civilization. On the third day she found a bigger waterway—but recognized at once that it wasn't navigable to boats, and was therefore unlikely to provide her with immediate help. By this point, the eggs that had been laid by flies in her wound had morphed into inch-long maggots, but Koepcke continued downstream, walking in the river, past crocodiles that dove into the water, and poking ahead of her footfalls with a stick to avoid deadly stingrays. On the tenth day after the crash Koepcke stumbled across a jungle hut and took shelter. Native lumbermen soon discovered her. They drove the maggots from her flesh with gasoline, then put her on a boat and took her to safety. She was the only survivor of the crash.

Expert Advice: When lost in the jungle, find a waterway and follow it downstream. Human settlements are most likely to be built near riverbanks.

Ten Must-Have Items in the Tropics

1. **Machete:** To clear paths
2. **Anti-malarial prophylactic drugs:** To ward off malaria
3. **Non-leather boots:** Leather is prone to rotting in moist environments
4. **Tobacco and salt:** Blend together into a leech-repelling paste
5. **Iodine tablets:** To purify stream water
6. **Twine:** For lashing; to hang food from tree branches away from your sleeping place
7. **Hammock:** Saves time and effort in creating shelter for sleeping off the ground
8. **Antibacterial soap and ointment:** Infections spread quickly in the tropics
9. **Rifle:** To hunt and defend yourself from animals
10. **Lighter:** Matches are likely to get waterlogged

LENGTH OF AMAZON RIVER VS. DISTANCE BETWEEN NEW YORK CITY AND ROME

Length of Amazon	3,969 miles
Distance between New York City and Rome	4,283 miles

Out and About

The Amazon River is full of hazards, but the candirú, also known as the "vampire" fish, is unique in its mode of attack. The candirú is a translucent, eel-shaped, parasitic fish that typically wriggles into the gills of bigger fish and uses its sharp spine to lodge itself inside as it feeds on the fish's blood. The candirú finds its host by seeking out the small currents formed when water exits the larger fish's gills, a current similar to the flow of urine from a human urethra. The inch-long fish can swim into a human vagina or penis and set its spike inside to feast on human tissue. The best way to guard against the resulting pain and a potentially fatal infection is to refrain from urinating while submerged in the water of the Amazon. Native peoples combine extracts of the Xagua plant and the Buitach apple to kill a lodged candirú and disintegrate its carcass, but immediate surgical attention is recommended.

HOW TO CROSS THE AMAZON RIVER

IF YOU ARE ALONE

1 Protect your feet.

Remove your socks, and lace up your shoes as tight as possible to shield your feet from rocks or sticks that could cut them and lead to infection. Shoes with sturdy soles offer the best protection against stingrays that may be found nestling in the river bottom. If you are wearing boots, tuck in your pant legs to reduce your resistance in the water.

2 Assess the depth and speed of the current.

The force of the current will be weakest where the river is at its widest. If the water is moving quickly and filled with stationary or moving obstacles, explore the area to find the widest point you can. Find a long, sturdy branch and probe the water from the bank to gauge the depth and force of the current. Fast-moving water higher than your knees can sweep you off your feet and carry you away.

3 Wear your backpack by the shoulder straps only.

Unfasten the waist strap to enable a quick jettisoning of the backpack in an emergency.

4 If wading is possible, use your branch to help you across.

As you work your way across, face upstream and use

the branch to help maintain your balance and to probe for underwater obstacles. Even a smooth, sandy bottom can conceal dangerous stingrays. Take small, incremental steps with the end of the branch leading your way along the bottom.

5 If the water is moving too quickly to wade, swim over the rapids.
In shallow rapids, lie on your back and point your feet downstream. Keep your arms close to your sides and use them like flippers to steer your body in the right direction. In deep rapids, lie on your stomach and swim diagonally across the river facing downstream. Do not attempt to swim while wearing a backpack.

IF YOU ARE TRAVELING IN A GROUP

1 Unfurl a length of rope about three times as long as the river is wide.
Tie the ends together to create a big loop.

2 Station two people about 20 feet apart on the riverbank.
Each person should hold onto the rope with both hands. One part of the rope will now be tight between them, and the other slack.

3 Send the first crosser through the river.
Direct the first person to cross to use both hands to grip the slack section of the rope midway between the two handlers and to hold on to the rope as he walks into the water. If the first person gets swept off his feet

Grasp the rope midway between the two people who will remain onshore and walk across the river.

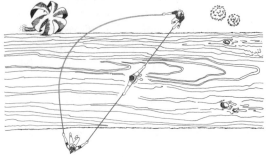

Pull the rope taut across the river as subsequent people cross. Allow the slack part of the loop to float downstream.

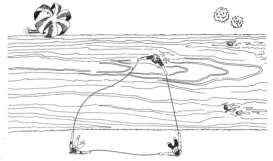

Station two people on the opposite side of the river to hold the rope as the last person crosses.

by the current, the other two should reel him back to shore.

4 Pull the rope taut across the river.
When the first person has made it across, he should pull on the looped rope to produce a tense length between him and one of the people on the opposite bank. The slack part of the loop will now be adrift on the river downstream from the taut part of the rope. This way, if subsequent crossers lose hold of the taut rope line, they have a chance to catch onto the slack line as a backup.

5 Instruct subsequent crossers to hold the taut rope line as they traverse the river.
Crossers should face upstream as they work their way across; it is easier to maintain balance this way.

6 When the last person is ready to cross, station two people about 20 feet apart on the riverbank's destination side, each holding onto the rope loop.

7 Bring the last person across the river in the same manner the first person crossed.

Be Aware
The best way to cross the Amazon is by raft, paddling across the river's widest point to avoid strong currents. Angle the raft slightly downstream so you expend your energy crossing the river rather than battling the current.

AMAZON RAINFOREST
"The River Sea"

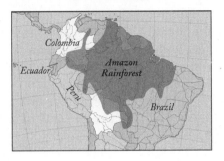

BEST KNOWN FOR: Habitat of millions of plant and animal species, many of which are deadly

LOCATION: 2.1 million square miles in South America, across parts of Brazil, Colombia, Peru, Ecuador, Bolivia, Guyana, Suriname, and French Guiana

DANGERS: Bushmaster snakes • Piranhas • Candirú "vampire" fish • Tigers • Leopards • Jaguars • Poisonous frogs • Acid-spraying ants • Malaria, dengue fever, yellow fever, filariasis

LITTLE-KNOWN FACT: Trees and plants in the Amazon rainforest supply more than 20 percent of the world's oxygen.

Number of insect species: 2.5 million • Number of reptile species: 378 • Number of amphibian species: 427 • Number of bird species: 1,294 • Number of mammal species: 427 • Number of fish species: 3,000 • Number of plant species: 40,000 • Pounds of living plant matter per square foot: 16

TWO SURVIVE TURBULENT TRIP THROUGH BOLIVIAN RAINFOREST

Israeli Yossi Ghinsberg, American Kevin Gale, and a fellow traveler employed the services of a non-native guide to lead them through the Bolivian Amazon. After hiking through the dense forest for several weeks without reaching their intended destination, the foursome decided to take what they thought was a route down the Tuichi River. They acquired a raft from some locals, but once they were on the water tensions quickly mounted as exhaustion set in. The guide abandoned Ghinsberg and Gale, taking the other traveler with him back into the forest. Neither man was seen alive again. Ghinsberg and Gale continued alone down the increasingly turbulent river until they reached the San Pedro Canyon, an unrunnable chaos of rocks and roaring whitewater that culminates in a waterfall. Just above the falls, the current pinned the raft against a boulder. Gale leaped to the riverbank, barely making it across—and dislodging the raft in the process. Ghinsberg went over the edge, disappearing into the depths of the river below for a full minute before popping back to the surface. He recovered a few supplies—including some food, a flashlight, and a first-aid kit—and struggled to the river's edge to wander alone through the rainforest. Leeches stuck to his skin. Quicksand sucked him into the ground until he escaped using swimming strokes. A jaguar stalked him until he sprayed insect repellent through the flame of his lighter, producing a ball of fire. After relying on his wits for 20 days, his determination paid off—a boat appeared carrying Gale and a local river pilot, and they ferried Ghinsberg to safety.

Expert Advice: Never enter the rainforest without an experienced local guide. Every jungle is different, and no amount of survival expertise can substitute for local knowledge.

SAILOR LIVES ALONE ON ISLAND FOR FOUR YEARS

In October of 1704, the buccaneer galleon *Cinque Ports* stopped at the uninhabited Juan Fernandez islands near Chile to refill its supply of freshwater. Sailor Alexander Selkirk asked to be left behind, fearing that the crippled vessel was on the verge of sinking. Selkirk's premonition proved to be well-founded—the boat later went down, taking most of its crew with it. Initially subsisting on a diet consisting entirely of shellfish, Selkirk was driven from the beach by a herd of sea lions during their mating season. In the jungle, rats nibbled on him at night, but Selkirk tamed a few feral cats to keep the rats in check. Previous visiting sailors had introduced goats to the island, and he caught them for milk and meat. The son of a tanner, he knew how to turn the animals' skins into clothing, and he used a nail to sew himself garments. He gradually learned to harvest the roots of native turnip plants. Despite having spent years alone on the island, Selkirk was able to restrain himself from approaching two Spanish ships that landed on his shore, realizing that his piratical background and Scottish citizenship would likely have earned him a painful death at their hands. Finally, in February of 1709, a friendly ship arrived. The privateers on the *Duke* landed in poor health, but Selkirk quickly trapped several goats to feed and revive his rescuers.

Expert Advice: Tropical islands are frequently home to introduced domestic animals that have gone feral. The benefits of taming them may outweigh their value as food.

HOW TO BUILD A MUD OVEN

1 Find a clay pot or metal canister, preferably with a lid.
If none is available, mold clay into a cylindrical cooking vessel and allow it to harden in direct sunlight. This may take several days or a week, depending on weather conditions.

2 Dig a trench in the firmest mud available.
Make the trench narrower and longer than your cooking vessel, about a foot deep, with walls as vertical as possible.

3 Place the cooking vessel on its side over one end of the trench.
Allow enough space underneath the vessel to accommodate a fire, digging deeper if necessary.

4 Prop a long, thick stick vertically against the bottom end of the cooking vessel.

5 Pack mud tightly around the vessel.
Fill in around the sides of the pot with an insulating mound. Make sure the stick still protrudes from the top of the mound.

6 Remove the stick to create a chimney.
The hole will allow steam and smoke to escape from underneath the pot.

Dig a foot-deep trench.

Pack mud around sides of vessel for insulation.
Put large stick in back of pot.

Remove stick, build fire, and cook. Prop lid on vessel with stick.

7 Build a fire underneath the cooking vessel.
Feed the flame with wood until the embers glow brightly.

8 Place your food inside the pot.
Wrapping the food in thick leaves will keep the food clean of mud and dirt.

9 Use a stick to prop the lid against the opening of the oven.
The container will be lying on its side; closing off the opening will maximize cooking efficiency.

10 Feed the fire as needed until the food has finished cooking.

FLOOD SEASON

Country	Rainy Months	Country	Rainy Months
Bangladesh	June to October	**Kenya**	March to May
Brazil	December to March	**Laos**	May to October
Burma	June to October	**Mozambique**	November to March
Cambodia	June to October	**Nigeria**	July to September
Colombia	April/May, October/November	**Peru**	December to March
Congo	October to May	**Senegal**	June to September
Costa Rica	May to November	**Sri Lanka**	October to January
Ecuador	September to June	**Tahiti and French Polynesia**	November to March
Guatemala	May to October	**Thailand**	June to October
Hawaii	November to March	**Venezuela**	April to October
Honduras	May to November	**Vietnam**	June to October
India	June to October	**Zimbabwe**	November to March

TREATING A POISONOUS SNAKEBITE

* **Wash the area with water and soap as soon as possible.** Do not try to suck out the venom or make additional incisions in the skin.

* **Keep the bitten area below heart level.** Do not tie a tourniquet to impede blood flow near the bite.

* **If possible, seek medical attention immediately.** If the snake can be killed safely, save it for medical personnel to identify.

* **If there is any question, proceed as if venom is involved.**

VENOMOUS SNAKES OF THE TROPICS

Name	Appearance	Geographical Range	Habitat
Bushmaster	Light brown body; very wide head	Central and South America	Rainforests
Cobra	Long body; spread hood	South and Southeast Asia, Africa, Middle East	Virtually everywhere
Death Adder	Brown/red body; lighter crossbars; triangular head	Australia	Bush, rocky areas
Eastern Tiger Snake	Olive or red body with lighter crossbars	Australia	Rainforest, grasslands
Fer-de-Lance	Gray/brown/red body with geometrical blotches	Central and South America	Rainforests, tree branches
Fierce Snake	Black markings on head; brown/olive body	Australia	Grasslands
Giant Black Tiger Snake	Black body; lighter crossbars	Australia	Sand dunes, beaches, grasslands
Mamba	Uniform dark color; very skinny body; small head	Africa	Rainforest
Tropical Rattlesnake	Dark stripes on neck; rattle at tip of tail	Central and South America	Dry, hilly terrain
Viper	Very wide head	Southeast Asia, Africa	Rainforest, grasslands

WOUNDED CONSERVATIONIST FENDS OFF PREDATORS AFTER PLANE CRASHES IN AFRICAN SAVANNA

While flying over Zimbabwe's Hwange National Park to track the movement of a rhinoceros, conservationist Greg Rasmussen hit a pocket of turbulence that stalled his ultra-light aircraft at 1,000 feet. The plane crashed into the African savanna 70 miles from the nearest road. Rasmussen awakened to the sensation of gasoline pouring onto his face. He couldn't move his legs, so he used his arms to push himself out of his seat and crawl away from the wreckage. He'd broken both femurs and several ribs, and shattered one ankle. He heard his pelvis crack as he tried to remove the boots from his swollen feet. Realizing that he hadn't issued a Mayday call, he dragged himself back to the radio only to discover that its battery had short-circuited. Hours passed. Then he heard elephants. Knowing the herd would panic and charge if they were surprised by a loud noise, he remained quiet, and the animals moved away. A lioness appeared, slowly advancing to within a distance of several feet. Rasmussen waited for the last possible moment in the lioness's approach, then he made a sudden loud noise by banging a piece of aluminum against the wreckage. The lioness retreated. Rasmussen watched the vultures circling overhead as he concentrated on taking deep breaths to infuse his diminished bloodstream with oxygen. Hours later a hyena found him, and he banged the aluminum once more. The next morning, hoping for a miracle, he tried the radio again. It had cooled overnight, and this time it worked. A rescue helicopter soon arrived and flew him to a hospital, where an eight-hour surgery saved his legs.

Expert Advice: When trying to scare off a predator with a loud noise, maximize the element of surprise by laying quiet and still until the last possible moment.

MOST DANGEROUS ANIMALS
IN THE SAVANNA

Species	Natural Habitat	Primary Danger
Cape Buffalo	Flood plains, high grasses, swamps	Ridged horns and brute strength
Elephant	Jungles, grasslands, bush	Stampede
Hippopotamus	Rivers, lakes	20-inch-long teeth
Hyena	Woodlands, semi-desert	Bite pressure can crush bone; prey is eaten alive
Leopard	Tree-lined riverbeds	Near-silent stalking technique
Lion	Grassland	Near-silent stalking technique
Rhino	Dense bush and short grassland	5-foot-long horn leading the charge
Wild Dog	Plains and bush	Dog packs can run 40 mph for as long as an hour

Out and About

There are only about 700 Bengal tigers in Bangladesh's Sundarbans mangrove forest, but the fierce animals kill as many as 80 people each year. One possible explanation for their penchant for human flesh is that frequent floods wash enough corpses into the swampy wilderness that humans have become a regular part of the Bengal tiger's diet in this area. Because the tigers prefer to attack from behind, local fishermen often wear backward-facing masks when trawling in the intertidal zone in an attempt to scare the cats away.

ELEPHANT DESTROYS JEEP IN SAFARI SHOWDOWN

In what would be the last trip the vehicle ever made, wildlife biologist George Wittemyer stopped his jeep about 300 feet from a pair of male elephants engaged in a fight for dominance. One of the elephants—dubbed Abraham Lincoln by the scientists in Kenya's Samburu National Reserve—was defending a challenge from an elephant new to the area. Wittemyer and his assistant watched as Abraham Lincoln delivered a devastating tusk blow to the newcomer's head. Apparently distraught over losing the battle, the defeated elephant turned its attention to an opponent it sensed it could conquer. Circling around behind the jeep, it cocked its head and drove its tusks right through the vehicle's fiberglass wall. With the elephant's head inside the vehicle, Wittemyer revved the engine and tried to drive away, but the five-ton animal pummeled the car violently against a nearby acacia tree, knocking the biologist's feet off the pedals and causing the jeep to stall. Subsequent blows snapped off a steel bumper and demolished the chassis. The elephant picked up the vehicle, turned it upside down, and smashed it on the ground. Several moments of calm ensued, during which a dazed Wittemyer discovered that his radio had gone dead. Then the elephant was back, charging the jeep again and flipping it back onto its wheels. Before the elephant could make its next move, Abraham Lincoln unwittingly saved the day, advancing on its rival and forcing it to retreat. Miraculously uninjured, Wittemyer and his assistant quietly exited the jeep, keeping the wreckage between themselves and the elephants as they darted into a stand of trees several hundred feet away.

Expert Advice: Stay quiet and still when you're at close quarters with an aggressive elephant. Sudden movements and noises may cause it to charge.

Out and About

Elephants kill 500 people each year, and casualties will only increase as humans and elephants continue to coexist in ever-closer quarters. As the human population grows, farms in Africa and Asia are encroaching on land previously inhabited only by elephants, leaving the elephants with less space to forage for food. In addition, humans have disrupted the animals' close-knit social structure, which depends on the stabilizing influence of the herd elders. Years of poaching and mass killings have eliminated many of the elephants that would lead today's herds. And because elephants have large brains and long memories, when a young elephant watches a human kill its parent or relative, it can develop a kind of post-traumatic stress disorder that brings a lingering aggression toward humans. Elephants can attack humans unprovoked, destroying huts full of sleeping people, goring with their tusks, striking with their trunks, and even rolling on top of humans to crush them. In the savannas of Africa, people are protecting their fields and themselves with a safe, nontoxic method: farmers are using capsaicin, the chemical that makes chile peppers taste hot, on hanging ropes and in "chile bombs." The elephants' sensitive trunks are irritated by the capsaicin and they learn to avoid areas where they may encounter the foul taste.

FROZEN STIFF

SHACKLETON AND CREW SURVIVE HARROWING EXPEDITION

Five weeks after setting sail for Antarctica on a 1914 expedition, Ernest Shackleton's ship *Endurance* got stuck in the churning icepack of the Weddell Sea, a stretch of ice and frigid water beneath the tip of Argentina. The British explorer had intended to lead his 27-man crew on the first crossing of Antarctica on foot, but his chances of success dwindled with each day the ship was lodged in the ice. Ten months after becoming trapped, the men heard the cracking of timbers as the pressure of the ice overwhelmed their boat. The crew abandoned ship, salvaging several lifeboats and their remaining provisions, and spent the next 23 weeks camping on a large iceberg, living on the meat of their 69 dogs. When the sea around them warmed enough for them to board their lifeboats, they suffered through a seven-day journey to the remote Elephant Island, but they were still so far from shipping lanes that they would never be found. Shackleton and five others set out again in hope of reaching a whaling station 800 miles away. Sailing through ferocious storms, knowing that a navigational error of just 2 degrees would cause them to miss the island and certainly perish, the skeleton crew miraculously reached their destination 17 days later. Following a strenuous trek over glacier-clad mountains, the men stumbled into Stromness whaling station and their salvation. Three and a half months later, after two failed attempts, Shackleton reconnected with the main party on Elephant Island. The entire crew had survived.

Expert Advice: Your best chance of polar rescue is from land; just because a ship can see you on the ice does not mean it can rescue you. When stranded in a large group, take advantage of numbers by using small parties to scout possibly dangerous means of rescue.

//

DIVE-BOMBING BIRDS

Beware of the large birds of the skua family, common to both the Arctic and Antarctic and well known for attacking humans with their hooked beaks and sharp claws. Skuas are hunters and scavengers that feed on fish, other birds, penguin eggs and chicks, and carrion of all kinds. They typically perch on high places and surprise humans by dive-bombing them from above. Their talons can easily pierce human flesh, though the damage they inflict is usually minimal due to the thick layers of outerwear worn by most arctic travelers. If you are attacked by a skua, prevent injury by beating it back forcefully with gloved hands.

//

Out and About

In the Arctic and Antarctica, objects may be much farther away than they appear. In most parts of the world, the higher you are from the earth's surface, the colder the air will be. But the extreme deep freeze of the polar icepacks can bring about the opposite effect. The subzero temperatures of the surface ice can supercool the air at ground level, making it denser than the significantly warmer air a few hundred feet above. Light passing from one atmospheric layer to the other gets bent and twisted, creating false images of islands that appear to float in the sky, or distorting natural features in the landscape, making a small hill look like a mountain. This effect sometimes even makes it possible to see things that lie beyond the horizon, as when light reflected at an upward angle off a distant object gets bent back earthward by contrasting layers of air.

Out and About

Though the Earth's two poles receive the same amount of sunlight every year, temperatures are significantly colder at the bottom of the world than the top. Because the North Pole is located in the middle of the Arctic Ocean, even during the winter when the ocean's center is covered with ice, the water beneath the ice is still no colder than 30°F. This relative warmth heats the ice from underneath and conducts heat into the atmosphere when ice patches part. By comparison, Antarctica is a giant land mass covered with ice more than a mile thick. The only liquid water to be found at the South Pole is in the containers brought by scientists and explorers—and even that water freezes in midair when shaken out of a canteen.

SIZE OF ANTARCTICA VS. AUSTRALIA

ANTARTICA   =   AUSTRALIA X 2

Antarctica	4.5 million sq. miles
Australia x 2	6 million sq. miles

ANTARCTICA

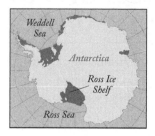

BEST KNOWN FOR: Extreme cold • Unforgiving, desolate environment

LOCATION: 4.5 million square miles of mountainous land covered in ice and glaciers at the southern pole of the planet

DANGERS: Winds of up to 200 mph cause exposed skin to freeze in minutes • No source of wood or fossil fuels for building fires • All-white environment without shadows makes depth perception impossible, causing inability to differentiate between vertical and horizontal

LITTLE-KNOWN FACTS: The ice on and surrounding Antarctica makes up 70 percent of the world's freshwater • The interior of the continent receives only about two inches of snow each year • Each person on Earth could have a chunk of ice larger than Egypt's Great Pyramid if all the ice on Antarctica was divided equally • The magnetic south pole is not located on Antarctica itself; it is situated 300 miles north of the Ross Ice Shelf

Average summer population: **4,000** • Average thickness of ice sheet: **7,200 feet** • Thickest part of ice sheet: **15,669 feet** (Wilkes Land) • Percentage of the world's freshwater contained in ice sheet: **70** • Average winter temperature, coast: **5°F** • Average winter temperature, South Pole: **-70°F** • Coldest recorded temperature: **-129°F** (Vostok, July 21, 1983) • Average summer temperature, coast: **30°F** • Average summer temperature, South Pole: **-20°F** • Hottest recorded temperature: **58°F** (Hope Bay, January 5, 1974)

HOW TO SURVIVE ON THE ICE UNTIL THE RESCUE PARTY ARRIVES

⭐ Wear several layers of loose clothing.
While exposure is the obvious danger in an arctic environment, you must also avoid *over*heating, which can lead to sweat that may freeze and cause hypothermia.

⭐ Breathe slowly, through one or more layers of clothing.
Very cold air inhaled too rapidly can damage the lungs and chill the entire body.

⭐ Keep all of your skin covered at all times.
Frostbite can kill human tissue in minutes under extreme conditions.

⭐ Protect your eyes with UV-blocking goggles.
Snow and ice amplify the effects of solar radiation, making snowblindness a real possibility. Keep your eyes covered at all times, even in cloudy conditions; just because the sun isn't visible doesn't mean that it isn't emitting harmful UV rays.

⭐ Melt snow and ice thoroughly before drinking.
Heating snow or ice in your mouth consumes valuable calories stored in your body and may elevate the risk of hypothermia. If you can't make a fire, use your body heat: place the snow or ice in a bag and insert it

*When walking across ice, hold a long pole parallel
to the ice at waist level.*

between layers of clothing. If you have the option, melt ice, which yields more water than a similar volume of snow.

★ Carry a long, sturdy pole while walking over ice.
Position the pole horizontally across your body, at belt level, as you move. Should the ice break beneath you, the pole may save you from falling all the way through into the frigid water below.

★ Remain constantly aware of the conditions of the ice and snow beneath you.
Dirty ice is weaker than clean ice of the same thickness since its dark color absorbs more heat from the sun. Snow-covered ice tends to be thinner than bare ice. In areas where there is a danger of avalanche, travel early in the morning, before the sun warms any of the snow and increases the chance of a slide. In mountainous terrain, snow often forms cornices that extend several feet from the lee side of ridges; these can easily break off when stepped on.

★ When crossing thin ice, crawl on all fours to distribute your weight.

★ Dig in during whiteout conditions.
Never travel during a severe storm, as you will quickly lose your way and expose yourself to dangers in the terrain that could be avoided if you were able to be more alert.

Build small, well-ventilated shelters.

Ice caves and snow trenches should be as small as possible to take advantage of your body heat, with holes for air to prevent suffocation. Never build a shelter out of metal, such as airplane wreckage, as it will whisk away whatever heat you generate. Don't sleep directly on the ground; create a layer of bedding made of fabric or grass to insulate your body.

SHIPS IN ICEBERG COLLISIONS SINCE THE *TITANIC*

Decade	Number of Collisions	Number of Sinkings
1912–1919	32	3
1920–1929	43	3
1930–1939	20	5
1940–1949	8	4
1950–1959	5	4
1960–1969	9	3
1970–1979	9	3
1980–1989	11	3
1990–1999	17	2

MYTH: For best results, always rewarm frostbitten tissue as soon as it is discovered.

FACT: Frostbitten tissue should not be rewarmed until you are sure the tissue will not refreeze—once tissue is frozen, there is not much more damage that can occur. Remove yourself to safety and only warm the affected area when there is no chance you will have to use it again in the freezing environment. To rewarm, immerse the frostbitten appendage in 105°F water, maintaining a consistent temperature—do not attempt to thaw more quickly, and do not use dry heat to rewarm, as burns may occur. Do not massage the thawing tissue, as you may amplify the tissue damage. Thawing is complete when color and sensation return. It will be very painful. Wrap the area with a clean cloth, insulate it from the cold, and refrain from using it until it has healed.

DETERMINING WINDCHILL AND FROSTBITE TIMES

Temperature (°F)

Wind (mph)	40	35	30	25	20	15	10	5	0	-5	-10	-15	-20	-25	-30	-35	-40	-45
5	36	31	25	19	13	7	1	-5	-11	-16	-22	-28	-34	-40	-46	-52	-57	-63
10	34	27	21	15	9	3	-4	-10	-16	-22	-28	-35	-41	-47	-53	-59	-66	-72
15	32	25	19	13	6	0	-7	-13	-19	-26	-32	-39	-45	-51	-58	-64	-71	-77
20	30	24	17	11	4	-2	-9	-15	-22	-29	-35	-42	-48	-55	-61	-68	-74	-81
25	29	23	16	9	3	-4	-11	-17	-24	-31	-37	-44	-51	-58	-64	-71	-78	-84
30	28	22	15	8	1	-5	-12	-19	-26	-33	-39	-46	-53	-60	-67	-73	-80	-87
35	28	21	14	7	0	-7	-14	-21	-27	-34	-41	-48	-55	-62	-69	-76	-82	-89
40	27	20	13	6	-1	-8	-15	-22	-29	-36	-43	-50	-57	-64	-71	-78	-84	-91
45	26	29	12	5	-2	-9	-16	-23	-30	-37	-44	-51	-58	-65	-72	-79	-86	-93
50	26	19	12	4	-3	-10	-17	-24	-31	-38	-45	-52	-60	-67	-74	-81	-88	-95
55	25	18	11	4	-3	-11	-18	-25	-32	-39	-46	-54	-61	-68	-75	-82	-89	-97
60	25	17	10	3	-4	-11	-19	-26	-33	-40	-48	-55	-62	-69	-76	-84	-91	-98

30 minutes   10 minutes   5 minutes   2 minutes

//

AVOIDING EYE INJURIES IN THE COLD

The extreme cold of the polar regions can freeze bodily fluids such as mucus and tears. Apply a bit of petroleum jelly to your eyelashes and the adjacent areas to prevent your eyelids from freezing shut. Do the same with your lips and nostrils, which easily become chapped. If your eyelids do freeze shut, cover your eye with your hand until the ice melts. In extraordinary conditions, the liquid in the eyeballs can crystallize into ice particles. Wear thick goggles to create an insulating layer of air between your eyes and the outside world. If your corneas begin to freeze, apply a hot compress or a warm hand until they have completely rewarmed, then cover both eyes with patches for two days to allow them to heal.

//

DOUGLAS MAWSON STUCK ON ANTARCTICA AFTER LOSING TEAM, PROVISIONS

While traversing the then-unexplored territory east of Antarctica's Cape Denison (due south of Tasmania) in November of 1912, expedition leader Douglas Mawson and his two companions were hit by a blizzard that temporarily buried their 12 dogs and camouflaged the terrain's hazards. After consolidating their provisions and discarding one sled, Belgrave Ninnis fell into a crevasse, taking his heavy sled and 6 dogs with him. Peering over the edge, all Mawson and Xavier Mertz could see was a single dog whimpering on a ledge next to an abyss. Mawson and Mertz shouted into the crack in the earth, but to no avail—Ninnis and the sled had disappeared, as had the lion's share of their food. Mawson and Mertz began feeding the remaining dogs mitts and rawhide straps. Then, one by one, they killed the dogs for food as they embarked on the 300-mile return journey. After eating the last dog, Mertz was seized by stomach pains that soon rendered him immobile. He died six days later. By this point, Mawson's toes were black with frostbite, but he pushed forward alone, through blizzards and without any remaining food, once even rescuing himself from a crevasse. Finally, 23 miles from safety, he spotted a cache of supplies left by a search party. By the time he made it back to Cape Denison, the boat he was supposed to take home to Australia was a shrinking blot on the horizon. He and the six men who had stayed behind with provisions would have to wait until the next boat landed—a full year later.

Expert Advice: When traveling in territory devoid of natural food sources, never store all of your provisions in a single place.

Ten Must-Have Items in the Arctic

1. **Rope:** For crossing crevasses safely
2. **GPS locator:** Often the only way to get your bearings—no landmarks to show the way
3. **Tinted goggles:** To protect eyes from snowblindness, freezing
4. **Emergency fishing hooks and line:** For ice-fishing
5. **Windproof parka:** To fend off winds of triple-digit speeds
6. **Ice axe:** For climbing slopes and stopping falls
7. **Snowshoes:** For traveling across soft snow
8. **Mylar emergency blanket:** For nighttime insulation
9. **Petroleum jelly:** Heavy-duty protection against windburn and chapping
10. **Snow saw:** For building ice and snow shelters

Out and About

If all of the ice in Antarctica were to melt, global
sea levels would rise about 230 feet.

HOW TO KEEP OCCUPIED DURING AN ANTARCTIC WINTER

⭐ Stay inside.
Antarctic winter temperatures average −76°F, with wind chill well below −100°F.

⭐ Engage in light therapy.
The 24-hour darkness of the Antarctic winter can cause Seasonal Affective Disorder (SAD), a condition with symptoms including general depression, emotional withdrawal, lethargy, extreme daytime sleepiness, inability to concentrate, carbohydrate cravings, and weight gain. To ward off SAD, sit several feet from a lamp 10 to 20 times brighter than average indoor lighting for 30 minutes a day until spring. Normal activities such as reading or eating can be performed while sitting near the light, as long as light enters the eyes.

⭐ Avoid medical emergencies.
Travel to and from the research station is impossible from mid-February to late October.

⭐ Do not plan to have a baby.
If you know you are pregnant, or you expect to become pregnant, leave the station by February.

⭐ Make friends.
You will remain with your colleagues at the station for a minimum of six months.

⭐ Avoid romantic liaisons.
You will remain with your colleagues at the station for a minimum of six months.

⭐ Appreciate the wildlife.
While pets are banned from the Antarctic continent, indigenous wildlife such as penguins and seals can temporarily provide the comfort of non-human companionship during your stay. Do not touch or pet the animals.

⭐ Drink in moderation.

Be Aware

* Frequent Antarctic blizzards cause massive snowdrifts and obscure visibility and cause whiteouts in the barren polar landscape, during which disorientation can occur easily in snowscapes with no landmarks or distinguishing features.
* If you experience feelings of depression, anxiety, fatigue, a craving for sweets, or weight gain, light therapy can reverse the symptoms.

Recognizing and Treating Hypothermia

Stage	Core Body Temperature	Symptoms	Treatment
Mild Hypothermia	95–98.6°F	Shivering, goose bumps, numbness in the extremities, difficulty performing complex tasks	Additional layers of dry clothing; generate heat with physical activity; increase fluid and food intake (especially carbohydrates)
Moderate Hypothermia	92–95°F	Violent shivering, difficulty walking in a straight line, uncoordinated muscle control, slurred speech, impairment of fine motor functions, depressed mood, irrational behavior (such as undressing)	Additional layers of dry clothing; generate heat with physical activity; increase fluid and food intake (especially carbohydrates)
Severe Hypothermia	86–92°F	Body stops shivering, frequent falling, skin becomes pale blue and/or puffy, dilated pupils, weakened pulse	Wrap in sleeping bags and layers of dry clothing; feed warm sugar water every 15 minutes to induce urination (preserving body warmth for vital organs); apply chemical heat packs or hot water bottles to the neck, arms, and groin
Imminent Death	75–86°F	Muscle rigidity, loss of consciousness, weakened respiration, erratic heartbeat, cardiac and respiratory failure	Concentrate on warming body's core by using a warm water bath or applying dry sources of heat; ignore periphery, which will dilate blood vessels and send cold blood back to the heart, causing heart attack

AMUNDSEN BESTS SCOTT IN JOURNEY TO THE SOUTH POLE

In the late southern spring of 1911, Norwegian explorer Roald Amundsen and Englishman Robert Scott set out on two separate expeditions to the South Pole, each hoping to be the first man ever to reach the destination. Both explorers had experience traveling in extreme conditions, but Amundsen had consulted native Arctic populations, which gave him a strategic advantage. The Norwegian put his faith in 52 sled dogs to haul his supplies and equipment, whereas Scott relied on Siberian ponies to pull his sledges. Amundsen's dogs sped along with relatively little difficulty, reaching the pole on December 14, after two months' travel. Scott's ponies, on the other hand, fared poorly in the broken terrain and harsh weather. After several weeks' journey, Scott's party was forced to shoot the animals and haul the 200-pound sleds themselves, uphill and over glaciers covered in soft snow. Although Scott and his men successfully reached the pole on January 18, the delays and extreme physical strain of the trip put his team in danger. While Amundsen and his crew were safely back at their base at the Bay of Whales, Scott and his team were fighting for their lives. Exhausted and lacking enough food for the return journey, Scott's men began to die as their rations diminished. Ten miles from one of the food depots they had created on the way out, a blizzard struck and pinned them in place. On March 29, 1912, Scott made his last journal entry. No one from his team survived.

Expert Advice: Always adapt your expeditionary strategy to the local environment. Talk to the locals or others familiar with the specific terrain you are traveling through for advice on how best to approach your excursion.

> **MYTH:** A shot of brandy will help revive hypothermia victims.
>
> **FACT:** Never give a hypothermia victim alcohol. Despite the old-fashioned image of a Saint Bernard dog coming to the rescue with a barrel of brandy around his neck, alcohol only intensifies the effects of hypothermia and causes the body to release its heat more quickly, rather than helping to generate it. Alcohol causes the expansion of blood vessels close to the body's surface, moving heat away from the victim's core and out toward the body's extremities and the surface of the skin. Treat hypothermia victims with warm (not hot) sugary drinks that are free of caffeine and alcohol.

//

FEEDING HYPOTHERMIA VICTIMS

Favor carbohydrates when trying to elevate a hypothermia victim's core body temperature. Carbohydrates contain five calories of energy per gram and release heat very quickly into the bloodstream. Proteins also contain five calories per gram but give off heat over a longer period of time. And though any food is better than none, at nine calories per gram, fats are the most energy-dense form of food, but they require water to metabolize, potentially increasing the risk of dehydration.

//

World's Largest Iceberg

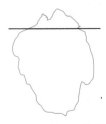

Name	Iceberg B15
Origin	Ross Ice Shelf, Antarctica
Birth date	March 2000
Length	183 miles
Width	25 miles
Height above water	120 feet
Depth below water	900 feet
Surface area	4,250 square miles
In comparison	The island of Jamaica is 4,244 square miles; 144 miles at longest point, 51 miles at widest point
Total volume of water	1,000 trillion gallons (i.e., 1 quadrillion)
Number of years it could have supplied the total freshwater needs of Europe	9
Most inconvenient resting place	McMurdo Sound, Antarctica, blocking supplies to McMurdo Station for 3 months
First breakup	Several pieces split away from the main iceberg in 2002
Last breakup	Largest remaining piece was driven aground and fragmented in 2005

HOW TO FISH ON THE ICE

1 Find bait or fashion a lure.

Small fish sometimes congregate near the surface in shallow waters. If the ice is thin enough to see through, drop a heavy rock and gather the fish that have been stunned. If finding live bait is impractical, make a lure by tying feathers from a bird or a down sleeping bag to the base of a fishing hook (or safety pin), camouflaging its barb.

2 Identify the best spot for catching big fish.

Large fish tend to favor deep pools. Investigate your surroundings to determine where the deep water is likely to be, such as on the outer banks of a bay. Remember that ice-fishing is like all fishing: some spots will be more productive than others for reasons that are difficult to parse.

3 Read the ice to minimize your danger of falling through.

Dirty ice tends to be weaker than thick ice. Snow-covered ice tends to be thinner than bare ice. Always avoid rocks or other objects that protrude from the surface of the ice; underlying currents and eddies can have a warming effect. When walking on river ice, stick to the inside portion of any bends; the faster-moving water on the outside of bends makes for weaker ice.

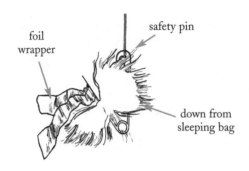

Use materials at hand to make a lure.

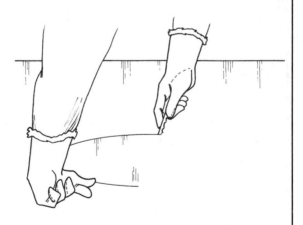

Carve a hole in the ice. If your knife is not large
enough, melt ice with fire.

4 | Cut a hole in the thick ice.
Use a saw or a long knife to carve out a hole in the ice. Never use a naturally occurring hole, which is likely to be surrounded by dangerously thin ice. If your tools are insufficient, build a small fire to melt a hole in the ice.

5 | Bait your hook.
If you are using live bait, insert the hook below the dorsal fin, making a hole beneath the backbone.

6 | Lower your line as deep as possible.

7 | Slowly pull the line toward the surface.
Jiggle it up and down as you raise it.

8 | If your hole is productive, keep it from freezing over when not in use.
Cover the hole with branches and snow. Check it routinely and chop through any new layer of ice that has formed.

Be Aware

- Make hooks of various sizes to maximize your potential catch. The sturdiest hooks are made from strips of metal or carved bone. Carved wood can also be used; season it over a flame to harden it first.
- When you catch a fish, investigate the contents of its stomach. If it contains freshly swallowed fish, save them as bait. Use partially digested food as chum, tossing it through your hole to attract more fish. Learn what the fish like to eat and try to bait your hook with similar food.

THE ARCTIC CIRCLE

BEST KNOWN FOR: Frigid water, polar ice cap, and islands and land-masses covered with snow, ice, and permafrost • Eskimos • Northern lights

LOCATION: Ice-covered ocean with a periphery of islands and land-masses in the earth's north polar region, including the Arctic Ocean as well as sections of Alaska, Russia, Greenland, Finland, Sweden, Norway, and Canada

DANGERS: Polar bears • Walruses • Summertime mosquito density up to 10 times greater than the tropics • Carbon monoxide fumes released by fires in unventilated shelters • Bloodsucking horseflies

LITTLE-KNOWN FACT: Harbors 400 native species of flowering plants

Average July temperature at the North Pole: 32°F • Average February temperature at the North Pole: -31°F • Coldest recorded temperature in the Arctic: -90°F, Oymyakon, Russia • Depth of Arctic Ocean: 13,000 feet • Thickness of the floating ice cap: 6.5 to 10 feet • First person to reach the North Pole: Robert Peary, April 6, 1909 • First crossing beneath the North Pole: U.S. atomic submarine *Nautilus*, 1958 • Most dangerous inhabitant: Polar bear • Most dangerous natural hazard: Flash floods during the spring thaw

SAILORS BUILD KAYAKS FROM SCRAPS, PADDLE THROUGH ARCTIC OCEAN SEARCHING FOR LAND

In October of 1912, the Russian exploratory vessel *Saint Anna* got trapped in Arctic pack ice. Although Siberia's Yamal Peninsula was close enough for the crew to explore it, Captain Georgiy Brusilov ordered the crew to stay with the ship, reasoning that the ship would move with the flow of the ice until summer's thaw. But summer failed to free the ship, and the ice pulled it 2,400 miles north over the next 18 months. On April 10, 1914, navigational officer Valerian Albanov decided to flee with 13 companions. Having scavenged wood, canvas, and spare metal from the ship, the group fashioned sleds and a pair of kayaks for their journey. They paddled through leads in the ice and hauled their crafts over the rough, icy surface. Food dwindled, and the men hunted seals and polar bears for meat. Walruses attacked their kayaks in frigid water. On June 25, Albanov finally sighted land—but he couldn't identify it. Using their harpoons as handholds to climb a steep glacier, the group reached a promontory full of bird nests and stole eggs to make omelets. Nearby they found a beer bottle that contained a note left by previous explorers, identifying their position. Armed with that knowledge, Albanov took to the open water again, paddling toward an old explorer's camp at Cape Flora in the Russian islands of Franz Josef Land. Losing one kayak in a storm and taking temporary refuge on an iceberg, the group was finally rescued by a passing ship 91 days after leaving the *Saint Anna*.

Expert Advice: If you are traveling in a kayak made partially from canvas, slather the fabric with seal fat to make it water-resistant.

//

TOXIC GUANO

Avoid gathering food in areas near Arctic seabird colonies. Arctic seabirds nest on the sides of cliffs in enormous colonies whose populations can surpass 20,000. The nutrients found in their feces support local plant life, and, in turn, the herbivores that feed on it. But seabird guano has an unusually dirty side: it often contains concentrated amounts of environmental toxins that move up the food chain, which is one reason why native populations in the Arctic tend to be overexposed to carcinogenic chemicals. Ponds beneath Arctic seabird colonies contain as much as 25 times more mercury and 60 times more DDT than ponds in bird-free areas.

//

SKINS AND FURS AS CLOTHING

Material	Advantages	Disadvantages
Seal Skin	Waterproof, hard to break	Not very warm
Polar Bear Fur	Very warm, waterproof	Heavy, inflexible
Musk Ox Fur	Very warm	Inflexible
Caribou Skin	Extremely warm	Hard to condition the hide
Arctic Fox Fur	Warm, soft, lightweight	Delicate, requires constant maintenance
Arctic Hare Fur	Warm, soft, lightweight	Delicate, requires constant maintenance

HOW TO BUILD AN IGLOO

1 Trace a circle on a flat stretch of hardened snow.
Make the circle about 12 feet in diameter.

2 Cut bricks of dry, densely compacted snow.
Using a saw or knife, carve about 50 bricks from the snow, each about 3 feet long, 1 foot high, and 8 inches thick. Cut some of them from one half of the area within your circle and the rest from a rectangular trench extending 6 feet from the near edge. The wall of your igloo will pass between these two pits, which you will later connect to create an entrance.

3 Arrange a layer of bricks around the edge of the circle.
Allow the bricks to lean slightly inward. Press the edges together firmly and pack snow into crevices and cracks.

4 Shave a diagonal cut from the top of the layer of bricks.
Use a snow saw to cut the bricks at an angle toward the center of the circle to enable you to stack the rest of the bricks in a spiral.

5 Stack bricks on the first layer to form the walls.
Stop building when the dome is halfway complete. Use snow to seal cracks and cement each new brick in place. Take your time; building an igloo is a slow process.

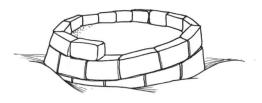

Shave a diagonal cut from the first layer of bricks.
Stack bricks on top to form walls.

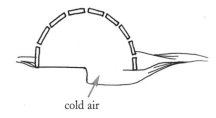

cold air

Cold air will sink into the lower level of the igloo.

The final square must be larger than the hole at the top.

6 Dig a tunnel through (or beneath) the foundation bricks.
When the dome is about halfway complete, create a crawl space that will serve as an entryway to the igloo. Connect the tunnel to the trench from which you cut your bricks to serve as a cold sink—cold air will fall to the bottom of the finished igloo, allowing you to sleep in comparatively warm air.

7 Build an elevated bed inside the unfinished dome.
Pile insulating materials atop the ledge where you did not cut any bricks.

8 Complete the dome.
Continue adding bricks until you reach the top. The last brick must be larger than the final hole at the top. Standing inside the igloo, shape it with your knife or saw until it nestles into the space.

9 Cut air holes in the walls of the igloo.
Carve one hole near the top and another near the entrance. Insufficient ventilation may lead to suffocation or carbon monoxide poisoning (if you build a fire inside the igloo). Check the holes regularly for blockage from ice and snow.

10 Build a roof over the entrance trench.
Use the remaining bricks to cover the entry, which will prevent snow from blowing into the igloo.

Be Aware

- Igloos are hard to construct, but offer a warmer, sturdier home than a snow cave. If there is good reason to believe that help will arrive in a day or two, consider saving your energy and building a more primitive shelter. If you will be on the ice for several days or longer, however, an igloo will repay your efforts with unbeatable protection from sun, wind, and cold exposure.

- The ideal snow for building an igloo is sturdy enough that you can stand on it without sinking but soft enough that you can insert a stick into it without difficulty.

- Even with a multi-tiered shelter and a fire, you will not be able to heat the air in the igloo warmer than a few degrees above freezing. However, the temperature inside will not drop below 0°F, no matter how cold it is outside the shelter.

- Keep plenty of food, fuel, and a shovel inside the igloo; if a storm blows in, you may be trapped inside for days and have to dig yourself out of the newly fallen snow.

- Stop drips in the walls of the igloo by packing new snow over the source.

- Knock loose snow off your boots and clothing before entering the igloo.

SEAMSTRESS SURVIVES TWO YEARS ON DESOLATE WRANGEL ISLAND

In September 1921, when Vilhjalmur Stefansson deposited Ada Blackjack and four male compatriots 80 miles off the coast of Siberia on the remote Wrangel Island, the 23-year-old Inuit woman thought he would return to take her back to Alaska in the summer. Blackjack had joined the Arctic expedition to serve as a seamstress for the men, who were claiming possession of the island for Great Britain. Blackjack and her companions ably lasted the winter, but their hope for a return voyage to Alaska faded as summer came and went. Despite strict daily rations, they exhausted their supplies quickly. The men managed to kill seals and polar bears during the first spring, laying in enough meat to stave off starvation, but the group still found their health deteriorating from scurvy. Hunting grew more difficult as the ensuing fall and winter arrived. In January of 1923, three of the men made a desperate bid to reach the Siberian mainland, taking a significant portion of the few remaining supplies with them. They were never heard from again. The fourth man became increasingly sick; Blackjack ministered to him until he died in June, leaving her to fend for herself on the island. She had never fired the camp's rifle or shotgun, but she soon learned to successfully hunt ducks, white foxes, and an occasional seal. In the wake of a narrow escape from a polar bear, Blackjack became increasingly frightened for her life. Finally, on August 23, 1923, the rescue ship *Donaldson* arrived and took the sole survivor of the Wrangel Island expedition back to Alaska.

Expert Advice: A diet lacking in vitamin C will lead to fatal scurvy. The best commonly available sources of vitamin C in the Arctic are the organs of sea and land mammals, preferably uncooked.

TRADITIONAL INUIT SOURCES OF VITAMIN C

Source	Milligrams of Vitamin C per 100 Grams*
Raw Whale Skin	360
Raw Fish Eggs	50
Raw Kelp	28
Blueberries	26
Caribou Liver	24
Ringed Seal Liver	24
Seal Brains	15

* Minimum amount required to prevent scurvy is 10 milligrams per day

Out and About

Caribou skin is a common clothing material among the Inuit because the hair on the skin is densely packed and each strand contains a tiny cell of air that boosts its insulation properties. However, before it can be made into clothing, the tough skin must be conditioned to make it more malleable. The traditional conditioning method involves chewing the skin until it becomes sufficiently soft—a task that typically fell to Inuit women.

WATER, WATER EVERYWHERE

Marine Creatures That Can Kill You Without Using Their Teeth

Animal	Habitat	Weaponry	Consequence
Box Jellyfish	Great Barrier Reef and eastern Australia	Dozens of tentacles as long as 10 feet, containing a deadly venom	Poison affects heart and lungs; can kill in minutes
Surgeonfish	Tropics and coral reefs	Razor-sharp spines in tail	Spines cause bloody wounds with high chance of infection
Rabbitfish	Coral reefs in the Indian and Pacific oceans	Venomous spines in fins	Poison can kill even after fish is dead and on butcher's block
Cone Shell Snail	Tropics and coral reefs	Harpoon-like barb	Barb injects a paralyzing venom powerful enough to kill a human
Barracuda	Tropical waters	Ciguatera toxin	Kills humans who eat flesh of infected fish

MYTH: A human can survive being swallowed by a whale.

FACT: In 1891, James Bartley created a sensation in Victorian London by claiming to have been swallowed by a whale and surviving after having been cut free from the whale's stomach. But the details of his story—the ship he said he was on was a cargo vessel, not a whaler, and there's no record of him having been aboard in any case—make it almost certainly false. Most whales feed on tiny plankton and other small marine life through a comb of thin plates of baleen, and their throat diameters are generally small enough to prevent swallowing an adult human. Sperm whales, which lack baleen, have much larger throats and have been caught with whole giant squid in their stomachs. Making your own way out of a whale is unlikely; many whales have complex digestive systems with up to four separate stomach chambers, and whale feeding also relies on a constant intake of seawater, meaning you'd almost certainly drown before making your way out.

//

MAKING AN EMERGENCY FLOTATION DEVICE

If you are thrown overboard and you are not wearing a safety vest, remove your pants and knot the bottoms of the legs. Wave them above your head to fill the legs with air, then push the waist under the water's surface to trap the air inside. Lean on the air-filled legs until help arrives.

//

WHALE CAPSIZES FISHING BOAT, SENDS FISHERMEN INTO STORMY OCEAN

On September 23, 2006, the 51-foot boat carrying Francis Redmiles and six of his friends collided with a 20-ton whale above the Atlantic Ocean's Wilmington Canyon, 65 miles off the coast of Delaware. Almost immediately, the cabin filled with a foot of water. In the seconds it took for Redmiles to grab his backup pump and dash back, the water had reached waist level. After radioing a frantic Mayday call, the seven recreational fishermen deployed the vessel's four-person tented life raft and crammed in. Five-foot waves grew to 9 feet and then to 15 as a storm descended, slamming the raft from peak to trough over and over as the evening wore on. Night fell. A cool breeze replaced the tempest and persisted through dawn. The men opened a compartment in the life raft that should have contained emergency food, but it was empty. Another day passed. One of the castaways became convinced that the raft was shrinking, and feverishly consulted the manual to figure out why. Evening brought another squall, but they held on through the night. The third morning's doldrums were broken by the thwapping blades of a Coast Guard helicopter. The men fired their final airborne flare in front of the helicopter's nose, but it peaked low, and the helicopter started to pass them by. They lit their last handheld flare and waved it out of view of the pilot, who suddenly decided that the "cloud" he'd passed might have been smoke. The helicopter turned around and the chopper team executed a rescue maneuver, strapping each of the castaways into a basket, one by one, and lifting them into the copter and then back to safety.

Expert Advice: Aiming a flare some distance from an aircraft will increase the pilot's chance of spotting you.

HOW TO SURVIVE IN A LIFE RAFT

1 Remain in the vicinity of the ship you've abandoned.

Rescuers answering an SOS message have the best chance of finding you if you stay close to your starting coordinates. Construct a makeshift sea anchor by tying a rope around the handle of a bucket or a roll of expendable clothing and secure the other end of the rope to the raft. Put the anchor in the water on the windward side to keep the front of the boat facing into the wind, making the raft less likely to capsize and minimizing the amount of drift caused by wind.

2 Use the wind to your advantage.

If you were not able to issue a distress call before you abandoned ship and you do not believe that help is on the way, improvise a sail. Tie two paddles securely to opposite sides of the raft, with the handles facing down. Stretch a sheet or poncho between the upright paddles. Use a third paddle as a rudder.

3 Read the clouds for signs of land.

Dense, puffy clouds with a flat bottom (cumulus clouds) in an otherwise clear sky usually form over land. White, fluffy clouds indicate good weather. A darker color spells rain. A greenish tint is known as "lagoon glare," which results from sunlight reflecting off shallow water, where it may be easiest to catch fish.

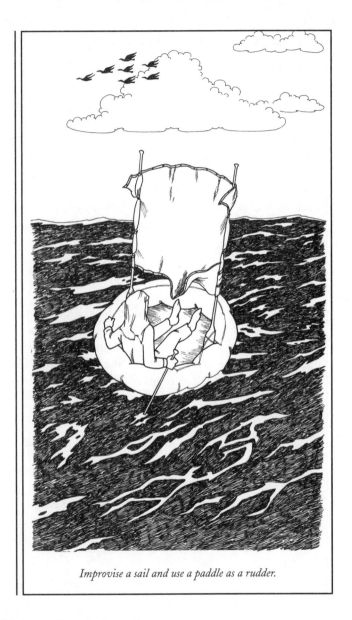

Improvise a sail and use a paddle as a rudder.

4 Let animals be your guides.

Seals in water are a guarantee that land is nearby, since they rarely venture far from shore. Single sea birds often leave land far behind, but flocks of birds are almost never more than 60 miles from the shore. They fly out to sea in the morning and return in the late afternoon to roost. Base your direction of travel on the time of day, heading in the opposite direction of the birds' flight in the morning and following them to shore in the evening.

Be Aware

- Do not drink saltwater directly from the ocean, no matter how thirsty you feel. Spread a tarp for collecting rainwater and dew. If the tarp is coated with dried salt, wash it off in seawater before spreading it; there will not be enough salt introduced by rinsing the tarp in seawater to harm you. Drink as much rainwater as you can to remain hydrated, especially when your freshwater supply is limited.

- Sunburn is a serious concern while afloat in the sea. If your life raft does not already have a roof, rig one using whatever material you have available and cover all exposed skin. Your face and neck are especially vulnerable and in need of protection.

- If you see sharks in the water near you, remain still and quiet. Do not put any body parts or equipment in the water. If you have a fish on the line when you spot a shark, let the fish go. Do not gut fish into the water when sharks are near.

BERMUDA TRIANGLE

"The Devil's Triangle," "The Graveyard of the Atlantic"

BEST KNOWN FOR: The disappearance of more than 170 boats and planes in its waters

LOCATION: 500,000-square-mile stretch of Atlantic Ocean between Miami, Puerto Rico, and Bermuda

DANGERS: One of few places on Earth where magnetic north and true north line up, causing navigational errors • The Gulf Stream causes tropical storms and hurricanes in the area • Methane deposits on the continental shelf periodically erupt, creating miles of frothy water without enough buoyancy to float a ship

LITTLE-KNOWN FACT: Marine insurer Lloyd's of London determined the area statistically no more dangerous than any other ocean expanse

Biggest ship lost: *Sylvia L. Ossa*, 590-foot German freighter, 1976 • Largest squadron of planes lost: five U.S. Navy *TBM Avenger* torpedo bombers, 1945 • Worst geopolitical consequence: USS *Epervier*, lost in 1815 while carrying the peace plan to end the War of 1812, thereby prolonging the conflict • Heaviest death toll: USS *Insurgent* in 1799, with a crew of 340 • Eeriest discovery: HMS *Rosalie*, found in 1840 completely vacant but in perfect condition

OCTOPUS TAKES ON THREE DIVERS IN UNDERWATER BATTLE

During a diving expedition in the South Pacific's Line Island chain, marine biologist Christine Huffard encountered an octopus with arms almost as big as hers. She tried to stuff the animal into her specimen bag, but the powerful octopus fought back, using its strong tentacles to wage battle against her. As two of her diving partners rushed to her aid, the octopus released a giant ball of ink into the water and clambered up the dive-safety officer's chest, completely enveloping his head with its arms. The octopus ripped the diver's air regulator from the mouthpiece he clenched between his teeth, making it impossible for him to continue breathing underwater. Huffard jammed her gloved hand between the octopus's sharp beak and her partner's head, which caused the octopus to release its grip. It shot off into the deep to escape. The dive instructor popped his backup regulator into his mouth, the divers regained their calm, and the team ascended to the surface.

Expert Advice: If you are attacked by an octopus, peel its arms from you one sucker at a time, beginning at the tip and working your way toward its center. If possible, attach the octopus's arm to another object so it will not immediately rewrap it around you.

MYTH: Urine neutralizes jellyfish stings.

FACT: Urinating on a jellyfish sting may actually release more toxins, making it even more painful. The burning, throbbing pain produced by a jellyfish sting comes from the release of venom from the stingers, or nematocysts, that attach to the skin upon contact with a tentacle. When urine or even freshwater are put on the nematocysts, the change in the concentration of salts can trigger the discharge of a second wave of venom. To effectively treat stings from the majority of jellyfish species, rinse a sting with saltwater, then soak a thin cloth in white vinegar and hold it on the sting for 30 minutes to deactivate the nematocysts. Once neutralized, make a slurry of seawater and sand, apply it to the affected area, and scrape the stingers from the skin using the edge of a flat shell, a credit card, or a safety razor.

//

RIP CURRENTS

- Before swimming at an unguarded beach, look for a long line of sandy or muddy water and debris heading out to sea, perpendicular to the shore.
- If you are caught in a rip current, swim parallel to the shore until you are free of the water's pull—a typical rip current is less than 100 feet across. Never attempt to swim directly to shore in a rip current; you will quickly tire and will not be able to fight the power of the current.

//

HOW TO EAT AT SEA IF YOU'RE ALLERGIC TO FISH

⭐ Test possible food sources for poison.

There is a wide variety of non-fish animal and plant life in the ocean, including sea cucumbers, sea urchins, and many varieties of snails. To analyze any potential food, place it on your tongue. If it stings your mouth or tastes revolting, spit it out. If the taste is acceptable, swallow a thimble-sized portion and wait one hour. Since most poisons produce symptoms in a short time, if you still feel fine, eat a small serving. If no symptoms occur within the next 12 hours, the food can be considered edible.

⭐ Eat seaweed.

Red, brown, and green seaweed are all excellent sources of protein, carbohydrates, iodine, and vitamin C. Dry thin leaves in the sun until they are crisp, then use them to flavor soups or broths. Thick varieties are best if they are washed in fresh water and boiled before they are consumed.

⭐ Make a bird trap.

Tie a loose noose knot with a piece of thin twine. Place fish entrails or another bait in the middle of the circle, then hold one end of the twine in your dominant hand. When the bird lands in the circle, cinch the line around its legs. Eat all of its meat and save the

PLANKTON NET

Remove arm from long-sleeved shirt.

Tie sleeve at wrist. Attach three strings to sleeve so it will open in the water.

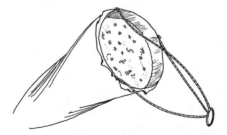

Drag net behind raft to collect plankton.

feathers, which can be used for insulation and fishing lures to catch more bait.

 Collect plankton.

Plankton is the foundation of the food web for a good reason: it contains protein, fat, and carbohydrates. If you are unable to find any other edible plants or animals, fashion a cotton shirt or another piece of permeable fabric into a net and collect and strain a remarkable amount of plankton from the sea. Remove all spiny material and stinging tentacles before eating. Exhaust all other food options first—it is easy to consume too much saltwater along with plankton, and depending on your location, there is a danger of ingesting poisonous dinoflagellates.

Be Aware

Shoe leather and other items of clothing are not viable sources of energy, even when you are starving. The human digestive tract is not built to process leather, and the nutritional value of fabrics such as cotton or wool is insignificant. However, the taste of leather bears enough similarity to overcooked meat that chewing on it may deliver a psychological benefit in truly desperate situations.

MAN SURVIVES 133 DAYS ADRIFT IN ATLANTIC

On November 23, 1942, a German U-boat patrolling the waters of the South Atlantic torpedoed the British merchant ship carrying Poon Lim, a Chinese sailor. Just before the vessel's boilers exploded, Lim donned a life jacket and plunged into the Atlantic Ocean. He soon found an empty wooden life raft, climbed aboard, and tied a rope from the boat to his wrist in case he fell overboard. As he exhausted the supply of biscuits, chocolate, sugar lumps, and drinking water he'd found tied to the raft, the 24-year-old castaway lost track of the days and began counting full moons. Faced with a lack of food, he used the few tools he had available to survive: he dug a nail out of the timbers of his raft and bent it into a hook for catching fish; he used the sharp edge of an empty biscuit tin to gut the fish he caught; and he collected rainwater in a canvas tarp. He maintained hope despite failed attempts at rescue, as when a freighter passed him by but declined to pick him up, and when a squadron of U.S. Navy patrol planes spotted him and dropped a marker buoy that was useless after a storm blew him far from that location. Four and a half months after Lim's saga began, he drifted into a Brazilian river inlet and was rescued by three fishermen. Having lost 20 pounds, Lim spent the next two weeks in a hospital before returning to England, where the British Navy updated its survival manuals with lessons from his ordeal.

Expert Advice: While drifting at sea, you are more likely to die of hypothermia or exposure than anything else. Cover yourself as best you can to protect yourself from the sun and wind, and stay out of the water, as prolonged exposure to seawater can damage your skin and cause lesions that are prone to infection.

EDIBLE PLANTS OF THE OCEAN

Name	Characteristics	Edible part	How to Eat
Sea Lettuce (Ulva)	Light green leaves with ruffled edges	Whole plant	Wash and boil
Dulse	Red or purple foot-long fronds attached to rocks	Whole plant	Raw, fresh or dried
Kelp	Olive green or brown fronds as long as 10 feet	Leaves	Discard leaf's dark membrane; boil middle section
Irish Moss	Bushy, anchored to rocks, color varies widely	Leaves	Boil; dry fronds in sun for storage

Out and About

In both the northern and southern hemispheres between 30 and 35 degrees of latitude, high-pressure belts called the horse latitudes drag sailing ships to a halt as the air falls to earth after rising from the equatorial zone. The weather becomes hot and dry, and dense air bears down with what sailors describe as a crushing weight. The name is thought to have originated from Spanish voyages to the New World, when galleons became trapped without wind for so long that the crew had to throw horses overboard to lighten their load.

WORLD'S WORST OIL SPILLS

Source	Year	Location	Amount (million gallons)
Kuwaiti Terminals, Tankers (deliberately released by Iraqi military)	1991	Kuwait, Persian Gulf	240
Ixtoc I Well	1979	Gulf of Mexico	140
Oil Well	1992	Uzbekistan	88
Atlantic Empress	1979	off Tobago, Caribbean Sea	84.2
Oil Well	1983	Nowruz Field, Persian Gulf	80
Castillo de Bellver	1983	off Saldanha Bay, South Africa	78.5
Amoco Cadiz	1978	off Brittany, France	68.7
Odyssey	1988	off Nova Scotia, Canada	43.1
Oil Well	1980	off Libyan coast	42
Haven	1991	Genoa, Italy	42
Torrey Canyon	1967	Isles of Scilly, U.K.	38.2
Sea Star	1972	Gulf of Oman	37.9
Irenes Serenade	1980	Navarino Bay, Greece	36.6

CAPTAIN AND CREW DEFEND LUXURY LINER FROM PIRATE ATTACK

While rounding the Horn of Africa on November 5, 2005, a cruise ship called the *Seabourn Spirit* encountered a flotilla of Somali pirates. At 5:30 A.M., a small fleet of 25-foot-long speedboats raced toward the 10,000-ton vessel, firing machine guns and lobbing rocket-propelled grenades, one of which penetrated an occupied luxury suite. Many of the 302 tourists on board were awakened by a public-address message from Captain Sven Erik Pedersen, who commanded, "Stay inside. We're under attack." The crew corralled pajama-clad passengers into the main restaurant in the middle of the ship while Pederson took an evasive maneuver, attempting to run over one of the speedboats and then quickly changing course in an attempt to outrun the marauders. Meanwhile, the crew raced to the deck to man the *Spirit*'s secret weapon: a sonic blaster. Developed by the American military to protect warships from small enemy craft, the satellite dish–shaped instrument emits sound waves powerful enough to knock assailants from their feet. Crewmembers triggered a series of thunderous claps and succeeded in preventing the pirates from taking over the cruise liner. One crewmember was injured by flying debris, but none of the passengers were injured.

Expert Advice: Keep cool and think methodically about the resources available to you in stressful situations.

HOW TO SURVIVE A PIRATE ATTACK

1 Once pirates have been spotted, take evasive action.
In safe water conditions, change directions radically.
Increase speed, heading for the coast if possible.

2 Let others know.
Transmit a danger message to ships in the vicinity.
Raise a distress signal on VHF channel 16 stating your
position—the effectiveness of assistance by shore-
based security forces depends on an early alarm.

3 Seal off access to the ship.
Attach rat guards to mooring lines and lock doors and
hatches.

4 Use water as a defensive tactic.
Spray water all over the deck to make it slippery, especially in areas where it is easiest for attackers to board.
Keep constant pressure in water hoses and consider
using them to repel attackers.

5 Use light and sound to confuse the raiders.
Shine lights into the eyes of pirates to blind them as
they scale the sides of your ship. Sound the alarm and
use intermittent blasts of the horn and rocket signals
to attract assistance from other ships. If necessary to
protect the lives of crewmembers, fire signaling rockets
into the pirates' access areas. Try to maintain control of
navigation without endangering life.

Douse deck with water to make it slippery.

6 | If your vessel is boarded, cooperate.

Allow the pirates to take what they want, minimizing the time they spend on board. Resist the urge to commit heroic acts—the faster the pirates leave, the safer you will be. Do not threaten to use firearms, which may provoke violent action from pirates with superior weaponry.

7 | Inform the authorities of the raid.

File a comprehensive report with the nearest Rescue Coordination Center. Notify the nearest coastal nation, as well as your ship's owners and flag state. Cooperate with subsequent investigation to help prevent future attacks.

How to Avoid a Pirate Attack

⭐ | Look busy.

The majority of attacks will be deterred if pirates are aware that they have been observed. Instruct crew members to move constantly around the ship, signaling to potential attackers that the crew is alert and prepared.

⭐ | Switch up your routine.

Make random rather than predictably timed patrols, preventing pirates from learning the ship's schedule.

⭐ | Strengthen night watches.

Increase the number of crewmembers on guard, especially at the stern between the hours of 0100 and 0600, when most pirate attacks occur.

⭐ Stay in constant radio contact with shore authorities and nearby vessels.

When passing through pirate-infested waters, maintain a 24-hour watch and establish walkie-talkie contact between lookouts and the bridge.

⭐ Make your vessel an unappealing quarry.

Remove valuable items from the deck, and use over-side and deck lights to illuminate the water and ward off potential raiders.

⭐ Do not engage locals who approach your boat in small craft.

What seems like an innocent attempt at trade may actually be a scouting mission for pirates.

Be Aware

Between 1984 and 2005, there were 3,992 documented pirate attacks. Modern pirates are most prevalent in the waters of Southeast Asia and the Far East, especially near Indonesia and Malaysia. Pirates also frequent the coasts of Brazil and Ecuador in South America, the Bay of Bengal and the Somali coast in the Indian Ocean, and the area around Nigeria in the Atlantic.

Out and About

Every year, an estimated 10,000 cargo containers fall off freighter ships, polluting the high seas with trash. In 1992, a container ship traveling from China to Seattle encountered a storm that sent 29,000 bathtub toys overboard. After bobbing to the surface in the middle of the north Pacific, the rubber duckies, turtles, frogs, and beavers traveled slowly toward the Alaskan coast.

In 1995, they reached the Bering Strait, passing between Russian and U.S. territory and proceeding beyond the Arctic Circle. Five years later, the toys reached Iceland. Some turned toward Europe, while others would soon be spotted near the waters where the *Titanic* sank 90 years before. Finally, in 2003, bleached white from more than a decade of sun exposure, a flock of hundreds of rubber duckies made landfall along the coast of New England.

ISLAND OF TRASH

Partial list of the 950 pieces of litter found by scientist Tim Benton in 1991 on a 1.5-mile beach on Ducie Atoll, a remote island more than 3,000 miles from the nearest continent and almost 300 miles from the nearest inhabited island. Ducie Atoll is an important breeding ground for seabirds.

Aerosol cans	7	Football	1
Asthma inhaler	1	Gasoline cans	4
Bottle tops	74	Glass bottles	171
Broken plastic pieces	268	Gloves (pair)	2
Buoys, large	46	Half a toy airplane	1
Buoys, pieces	66	Jars	18
Buoys, small	67	Light bulbs	6
Can of meat	1	Pieces of plastic pipe	29
Cans of food/drink	7	Pieces of rope	44
Car floor mat	1	Plastic bottles (drinks, toiletries)	71
Cigarette lighters	3	Plastic coat hanger	1
Construction worker's hat	1		
Copper sheeting from shipwrecks	8	Pop tops	2
		Shoes	25
Crates (bread, bottle)	14	Tea strainer	1
Dolls' heads	2	Toy soldier	1
Fluorescent tubes	6	Truck tire	1

DEEPEST OCEAN CHASMS

Abyss	Depth	Ocean
Mariana Trench	35,797 feet	Northwest Pacific
Mindanao Deep	35,597 feet	West Pacific
Kuril-Kamchatka Trench	34,449 feet	Northwest Pacific
Kermadec Trench	32,963 feet	South Pacific
Tonga Trench	32,480 feet	Central Pacific
Japan Trench	29,527 feet	West Pacific
Milwaukee Deep	28,232 feet	West Atlantic
Puerto Rico Trench	27,559 feet	West Atlantic
Peru-Chile Trench	26,456 feet	East Pacific
Cayman Trench	25,216 feet	Caribbean

Pressure at the Bottom of the Deepest Ocean Chasm

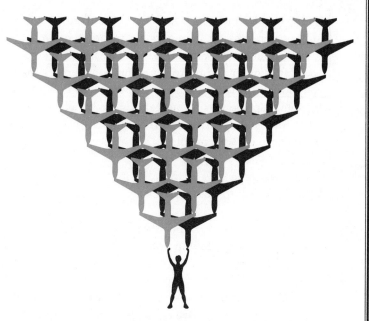

Pressure at Challenger Deep, a point 36,201 feet below sea level in the Mariana Trench, the lowest place on Earth:
8 tons per square inch; weight of 48 jumbo jets

HOW TO FLIP AN OVERTURNED KAYAK

1 Bend forward at the waist.

Being upside down in a kayak puts your entire torso underwater, making it impossible to breathe. Do not thrash about in the water, which is only likely to empty your lungs of air and make your situation worse. When your kayak overturns, curl at the waist and count to three to help you regain your calm as the kayak naturally aligns in a stable position in the turbulent water. Keep a tight grip on your paddle.

2 Lean toward the left side of the boat.

Flex at the hip to hold yourself in position.

3 Line up your paddle parallel to the kayak.

Hold the paddle firmly in both hands.

4 Sweep the paddle blade away from the boat.

With your right hand, which will be closest to the bow (front) of the kayak, move the paddle outward, keeping it just beneath the surface of the water.

5 Lean upward.

Move your head and torso as close to the surface as possible, resisting the urge to pull your head completely out of the water.

6 Snap your hips to flip the kayak.

As your sweeping paddle motion is midway to completion,

Sweep the paddle away from the boat, moving your head and torso closer to the surface.

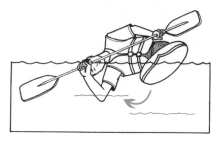

Rotate your hips so you are leaning all the way to the right.

As the kayak rights itself, pull your shoulders and head back into an upright position.

quickly snap your hips in one fluid motion so that instead of leaning your torso all the way toward your left side, you will be leaning all the way to the right as the kayak comes underneath your center of gravity. The friction of your paddle in the water will combine with the hip snap to create enough momentum to flip the boat partially onto its keel. Your head and torso will still be touching the water's surface.

7 Recover your stability.

In a fluid continuation of the flip, bend your torso out of the water, using your legs and abdominal muscles to bring the kayak closer to your head. As the kayak begins to sit upright in the water, whip your head from the water surface and sit up straight.

Be Aware

- Kayaks flip easily in turbulent water. If you are not confident in your kayaking skills, or if you lack experience in fast-moving water, practice flipping the kayak over in still water until you gain confidence.

- Wear a nose-clip when kayaking in choppy water to pinch your nostrils together and prevent water from rushing into your nasal passages.

Out and About

Water conducts heat about 25 times more efficiently than air, which is why hypothermia and wetness often go together. Even warm water can lower your body temperature to a dangerous level.

SURVIVAL TIME IN WATER

Water Temperature	Loss of Dexterity	Exhaustion/ Unconsciousness	Estimated Survival Time
32.5°F	Less than 2 minutes	Less than 15 minutes	15–45 minutes
32.5–40°F	Less than 3 minutes	15–30 minutes	15–90 minutes
40–50°F	Less than 5 minutes	30–60 minutes	30 minutes–3 hours
50–60°F	10–15 minutes	1–2 hours	1–6 hours
60–70°F	30–40 minutes	2–7 hours	2–40 hours
70–80°F	1–2 hours	2–12 hours	3 hours+
Over 80°F	2–12 hours	Unlikely	Indefinite

//

SURVIVING IN THE DOLDRUMS

When crossing the equator in a sailing vessel, stock your craft with at least two more weeks of food than you expect you'll need for your journey. For several degrees of latitude on either side of the equator, in an area called the Doldrums, the trade winds of the southern and northern hemispheres cancel each other out, preventing a prevailing wind from establishing itself. Intense solar radiation heats up the surface waters in this zone, so the predominant direction of air movements isn't east, west, south, or north, but straight up. When the breeze dies in the Doldrums, there's no telling when it will resurrect itself.

//

Out and About

On July 16, 1998, Benoit Lecomte waded into the ocean near Hyannis, Massachusetts, and began swimming east. Seventy-two days later, the 31-year-old adventurer pulled himself out of the water in Quiberon, France, becoming the first human to cross the Atlantic Ocean using nothing more than his arms and legs. Although a boat followed along, allowing Lecomte to eat and sleep during his voyage, he ultimately swam about 3,700 miles to raise funds for cancer research.

How Many Laps Is That?

English Channel
4,800 laps

Atlantic Ocean
96,000 laps

Indian Ocean
198,400 laps

Pacific Ocean
393,150 laps

MEAN STREETS
AND MALLS

World's Most Densely Populated Cities and Urban Areas

Rank	City/Urban Area	Population	Density (people per sq. km)
1	Mumbai, India	14,350,000	29,650
2	Kolkata, India	12,700,000	23,900
3	Karachi, Pakistan	9,800,000	18,900
4	Lagos, Nigeria	13,400,000	18,150
5	Shenzhen, China	8,000,000	17,150
6	Seoul/Incheon, South Korea	17,500,000	16,700
7	Taipei, Taiwan	5,700,000	15,200
8	Chennai, India	5,950,000	14,350
9	Bogota, Colombia	7,000,000	13,500
10	Shanghai, China	10,000,000	13,400
11	Lima, Peru	7,000,000	11,750
12	Beijing, China	8,614,000	11,500

HOW TO AVOID GETTING MUGGED WHILE WALKING IN THE PARK

⭐ Avoid the park at dangerous times.
Do not enter the park at times of decreased visibility, from dusk to dawn, or sparsely populated times, such as during bad weather or extreme temperature. Avoid the park when it is particularly crowded.

⭐ Avoid foliage.
Trees with large trunks, hedges, and areas of tall grass or brush can provide cover for potential muggers.

⭐ Avoid structures.
Maintenance sheds, restrooms, snack bars, museum buildings, ice skating rinks, and merry-go-rounds can provide cover for potential muggers.

⭐ Avoid people.
Be wary of anyone who approaches you, especially if they are smiling. Be wary of anyone who is walking at a constant distance from you but does not approach you. Be wary of groups of people.

⭐ Avoid sitting down.
If you do sit, do not remain seated if someone approaches.

Clutch your bag tight, in front of your body.
Avoid people, foliage, structures, and sitting down.

⭐ Look confident.

⭐ Walk purposefully.

⭐ Do not make eye contact.

⭐ Keep one hand in your pocket to give the impression you may be armed.

⭐ Never count your money in public.

How to Protect Your Money

⭐ Carry a fake wallet.
Keep a small amount of cash and a gift card that looks like a credit card in the wallet. Give it to a mugger rather than handing over your real wallet.

⭐ Hide your real wallet.
Wear your wallet around your neck, under your clothes.

⭐ Carry your purse or backpack in front of you rather than on your side or back.
Do not carry any handbag that cannot be closed completely. Keep your wallet pushed down inside your purse, preferably inside a zipped compartment.

⭐ Keep some spending money outside your wallet.
Put a small amount of cash in your front pocket so you don't have to access your wallet for small transactions.

⭐ Only use ATMs located inside of bank buildings.

CONSTRUCTION WORKER DROPS TWO STORIES INTO POOL OF WET CEMENT, SURVIVES

While mixing cement on a construction site in Singapore in 1999, Chen Guo Chang felt the scaffolding give way beneath his feet. Before he could make sense of what was happening, his body was in free fall—he dropped two stories down into a deep pool of wet cement. The force of Chang's plunge drove him deep into the dense mixture, injuring his spine and rendering his left arm immobile. The 36-year-old closed his eyes and screamed for help between panicked gasps for air. Chang could still move his right arm, which he used to wipe cement from his face—though he couldn't avoid swallowing some cement as he struggled to breathe. A number of other workers had also sustained injuries from the platform's collapse, so Chang fought to keep his face above the surface for an agonizing and exhausting 30 minutes before rescuers found him and managed to extricate him.

Expert Advice: When working around wet cement, always keep extra plywood on hand in case of an emergency. Plywood can help you to work your way to safer ground and provide a means for rescuers to reach you more easily, too.

HOW TO SURVIVE A FALL INTO A POOL OF WET CEMENT

1 Keep your body upright.

The high density of the cement will prevent you from sinking very far down into the pool. If your head is under the cement, use your legs and arms to push yourself above the surface as you would if you were underwater.

2 Yell for help.

Shout until the workers pouring the cement have cut off the flow.

3 Keep your eyes and mouth closed.

Cement contains lime or other alkaline compounds that will burn skin with prolonged contact. Sensitive tissue, such as the eyes, nasal passages, and mouth, are especially vulnerable. If opening your eyes may put cement in direct contact with your eyeballs, keep at least one eye closed at all times, and open the other only to determine which direction you should move to get to safety.

4 Use a freestyle swimming stroke to move toward safety.

If the cement is wet and deeper than you are tall, keep your head above the surface and push the cement away from you as though you are swimming.

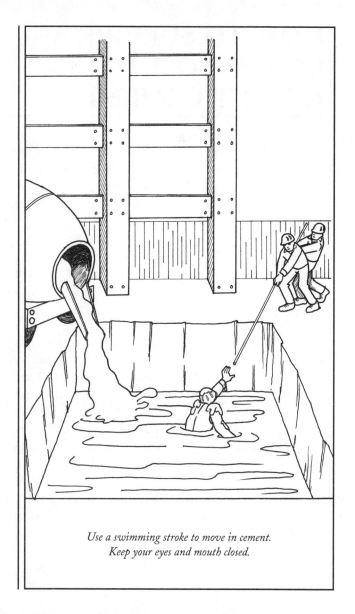

Use a swimming stroke to move in cement.
Keep your eyes and mouth closed.

5 If you are unable to move, instruct bystanders to pour sugar into the cement.

Sugar slows the chemical reaction that causes cement to harden. Adding sugar to the cement will buy time and make it safer for rescue personnel to extract you.

6 Remove cement-covered clothing.

As soon as possible, take off all clothes that contacted cement, including socks, underwear, and hats. Prolonged contact with the skin can result in third-degree burns or skin ulcers, necessitating hospitalization and skin grafts. Cement burns can happen painlessly, so you may not even know you've been hurt until severe skin damage has occurred.

7 Wash thoroughly.

Vigorously wash the burn with soap and water. Rinse all skin that came in contact with cement for at least 30 minutes.

8 Seek professional medical attention.

Cement burns can be worse than they first appear. Visit a doctor to see if additional treatment is required.

Bad Air

* **Avoid exercising near major thoroughfares.** Automobile exhaust is a major source of air pollution. Aerobic exercise in areas with heavy traffic draws airborne toxins deep into the lungs.

* **Stop smoking cigarettes.** Living amidst heavy air pollution elevates your risk of respiratory disease, and smoking exacerbates the injuries your lungs are already sustaining.

* **Reduce the use of fireplaces and wood-burning stoves.** When the outside air is heavily polluted, keeping the air inside your home as clean as possible is vital to your health.

* **Eat a diet high in raw vegetables and fresh fruit and low in saturated fat.** Medical research indicates that raw vegetables and fruit decrease the risk of lung cancer in nonsmokers.

* **Eat plenty of grains, seeds, and fish.** These foods are high in selenium, a mineral that is beneficial to the health of lung tissue.

* **Take regular vitamin and antioxidant supplements.** Vitamins A, C, E, and beta-carotene have been shown to protect the body from the effects of ozone and other components of air pollution.

* **When there is an elevated level of fine particulate pollution in the air, wear a surgical mask.** Sources of fine particulate pollution range from automobile exhaust to building demolitions. When the air is visibly laden with fine particles, breathe through a mask or a layer of natural fiber such as cotton.

LOOK BOTH WAYS

Pedestrians killed after being hit by motor vehicles in 2003

USA	🚶🚶🚶🚶🚶🚶🚶🚶🚶🚶🚶🚶🚶🚶🚶🚶	3,101
JAPAN	🚶🚶🚶🚶🚶🚶🚶🚶🚶🚶🚶🚶🚶🚶	2,650
POLAND	🚶🚶🚶🚶🚶🚶🚶🚶	1,530
EGYPT	🚶🚶🚶🚶🚶	901
BRAZIL	🚶🚶🚶	611
COLOMBIA	🚶🚶🚶	504
GERMANY	🚶🚶	471
HUNGARY	🚶🚶	413
MEXICO	🚶🚶	298
ROMANIA	🚶🚶	270

Out and About

In 1896, Bridget Driscoll died after being hit by a car in Crystal Palace, London. She was the first pedestrian to suffer a fatality from a collision with a motorized vehicle, prompting the comment "This must never happen again" from the coroner in charge of the inquest of her death. Today, pedestrians account for almost half the traffic-related deaths in London.

MOST POLLUTED CITIES ON EARTH

City	People Affected	Problem
Chernobyl, Ukraine	More than 5.5 million	Radiation from nuclear melt-down in 1986
Dzerzhinsk, Russia	300,000	Water contaminated with more than 300,000 tons of chemical waste from former chemical weapons plant, including Sarin, VX gas, arsenic, mustard gas, dioxins, and phenol
Haina, Dominican Republic	85,000	Soil contaminated with lead from former car battery recycling smelter
Kabwe, Zambia	250,000	Soil and water contaminated with lead and cadmium from former mining and smelting operations
La Oroya, Peru	35,000	Toxic emissions from poly-metallic smelter, bringing lead, copper, zinc, and sulfur dioxide contamination
Linfen, China	200,000	Air filled with stifling coal dust; worst air quality in China; lead and arsenic poisoning
Mailuu-Suu, Kyrgyzstan	23,000, possibly millions	Radioactive mine waste from former uranium plant
Norilsk, Russia	134,000	More than 4 million tons of cadmium, copper, lead, nickel, arsenic, selenium, and zinc released into air annually from world's largest heavy metal smelting complex
Rudnaya Pristan, Russia	90,000	Water, air, and soil contaminated with lead from former smelter and unsafe transport of lead from mine
Ranipet, India	3.5 million	Groundwater contaminated with waste from leather tannery

CITIZENS GENERATE OWN POWER

During the war in Bosnia in the early 1990s, the United Nations–designated "safe area" in Gorazde lost its source of electrical power when Serbian forces took control of the nearby hydroelectric plant. With scrap materials and ingenuity, the townspeople set up an alternative system to keep their lights on. They attached home-built paddle wheels to wooden platforms and mounted the contraptions on barrels that served as flotation devices. The main body of each platform housed an electrical generator yoked to the paddle wheel. Taking advantage of the bridge across the Drina River, which ran through town, they deployed these miniature power plants atop the moving current, anchoring them to the overpass with ropes. Wires were strung from the paddle-wheel generators to the bridge and then to individual homes. With frequent maintenance to ensure that the gears were moving properly and the paddles remained free of driftwood and river detritus, the generators produced a steady but modest stream of electricity. Depending on the volume of water passing under the bridge, the wires occasionally carried enough juice to allow the besieged citizens to watch television or even movies on VCRs. Natural fluctuations in the current caused sudden power surges and outages, but an irregular supply of electricity was better than none at all.

Expert Advice: Incorporating energy-generating systems, such as solar panels, into your home decreases your vulnerability to power-grid catastrophes.

HOW TO SURVIVE A POWER OUTAGE IN THE SUBWAY

1 Stay alert.

As your eyes adjust to the darkness, press your bag, purse, or other possessions against your body and move your hand near your wallet or other valuables. A generator is likely to turn on, and emergency lighting will be activated.

2 Press the emergency call button.

Tell the subway official that there are people on your car, and inform her of any special rescue considerations (for instance, if someone on your car is confined to a wheelchair or otherwise unable to walk on their own).

3 Listen for an announcement on the public address system.

Transit officials should provide you with instructions for maintaining your safety. If the PA system is not working, a member of the crew will walk through the train to tell passengers the emergency evacuation procedures.

4 Stay on the train.

Do not leave the train until a transit officer or crew member advises you to do so. The power could be restored at any moment, electrifying the track's third rail to allow the trains to start moving again but endangering those walking on the tracks. You will expose yourself to greater danger by leaving the train without the assistance of trained personnel than you will in the relatively protected subway car.

5 | Open the emergency windows.
The lack of electricity may prevent the ventilation system from working properly, so open the windows on the car to encourage circulation.

6 | Tie your shoelaces in tight double knots.
If the transit officials determine that evacuation is necessary, pull your socks up as high as possible on your legs and secure your shoes on your feet. The tunnels you will be walking through will be grimy and germ-laden and may hold inches of water that could pull your shoes from your feet.

7 | Follow transit workers' evacuation instructions.
Every subway system has its own emergency evacuation procedures, and its crew members are trained to execute them. In power outages, many passenger evacuations occur in the drainage trough between the rails or along a benchwall, an elevated platform that runs adjacent to the train. In both cases, you will be led to the nearest emergency exit or station platform.

8 | Stay away from the third rail.
Locate the track's third rail and keep as far away from it as possible. Technicians should have ensured that restored electricity won't flow through the rail while passengers are on the track, but be cautious nonetheless.

MAN DIVES ONTO SUBWAY TRACKS TO RESCUE SEIZURE VICTIM

Wesley Autrey, a construction worker from Harlem, New York, was waiting for a downtown subway train when 19-year-old Cameron Hollopeter fell to the ground in a seizure. Autrey and two others stood by him to offer assistance, and Hollopeter soon recovered enough to stand up. But just as the crowd on the platform detected the approach of an oncoming train, Hollopeter once again lost control of his body, and this time he fell down onto the tracks. A moment later Autrey jumped down after him, intentionally putting himself in the train's path so he could save the disoriented man's life. Autrey wrapped his arms around Hollopeter, pushed him into the drainage area between the rails, and laid on top of him, pinning his still-seizing arms and legs underneath his own body as the train screeched to a halt with just two inches of clearance between the train's undercarriage and Autrey's back. Two train cars rushed over them before the train finally stopped, trapping them there, face to face, for more than 20 minutes as transit technicians turned off the power to the third rail. Both men escaped serious injury, and Autrey emerged as New York's newest hero, for which he received extensive media attention, a Bronze Medallion from the City of New York, a special mention in President George W. Bush's 2007 State of the Union Address, and a year's worth of free rides on New York's transit system.

Expert Advice: If you fall into the path of an oncoming subway train, your best escape option is to stand next to a pillar between two sets of tracks. Lie down between the tracks only as a last resort—there may not be enough clearance between your body and the train, or the train may be dragging something that could injure you.

Tokyo's "Commuter Hell"

* **Travel in off-peak hours.** The Tokyo subways serve more than 8 million commuters each day, and during rush hour subway cars can be packed to as high as 197 percent capacity. The busiest hours are from 7 to 9:30 A.M. and from 4:30 to 7:00 P.M. The trains fill up again at midnight, just before they stop running for the night.

* **Line up in designated areas.** A station employee will likely direct you to waiting areas demarcated for each car of the train.

* **Beware of disembarking passengers.** Do not stand directly in front of the train doors when it opens to discharge passengers. You will be pushed, knocked down, or trampled by the crowd.

* **Use your bag as a shield.** After the disembarking passengers have stepped onto the platform, hold your bag at face level about a foot in front of you and push your way onto the train. Look down at the ground; do not make eye contact with other passengers.

* **Wedge yourself into a corner.** Twist, turn, and push your way through the other passengers and squeeze yourself into the corner formed by the intersection of the seats and the wall of the car. Do not stop in the middle of the aisle where you cannot reach an overhead bar or handstrap, or you risk falling onto fellow passengers when the train starts and stops.

* **Turn your back to the crowd.** Once you are in the corner, you will be sheltered from the other passengers on three sides.

* **Put your bag between your feet.** Stand with your feet shoulder-distance apart and place your bag on the floor between them. Keep your feet against the bag at all times to deter thieves.

* **Start for the door one stop before your actual destination.** Give yourself time to make your way through the crowd so you don't miss your stop.

//

PREVENTING FIRE AT THE GAS PUMP

Gasoline fumes are volatile, and each time you refuel your car you are exposing yourself to the potential for a fire. The friction created when your clothing rubs against the seat of your vehicle can produce a charge like the shock you feel when you touch something metal after dragging your feet on carpeting. If a static spark is released when you touch a metal fuel nozzle, gasoline vapors can ignite and cause a fire. To reduce the risk of fire, touch the metal part of the door as you exit the vehicle to discharge any built-up static electricity before you begin fueling. Never get back into your vehicle while refueling is in process.

//

Out and About

China's rural roads are highly trafficked and often highly congested, so much so that one- or two-day jams are not unusual. But in August 2004, Route 307 across the provinces of Shanxi and Hubei clogged in a 60-mile jam that lasted for 10 entire days. Thousands of passengers stayed with their vehicles through downpours and extreme heat. The jam was blamed on an increase in traffic coupled with road construction.

How to Tell Which
Tract Home Is Yours

* **Engage your remote garage door opener.** Drive down the street you think might be yours and press your garage door opener in front of each house that looks like yours. Use your peripheral vision to watch the garage doors of neighboring houses, as the range for a typical remote extends 150 feet.

* **Examine the contents of the garage.** Not recognizing the things in the garage does not necessarily mean the house is not yours.

* **See if children or pets playing in front of house are yours.** If you do not know the children, ask them if they have recently seen your son or daughter. Read their reactions to determine whether your own children may be inside the house.

* **Check the mailbox.** Is the name on the box yours? Do the numbers match your address? Open the box and pull out an envelope. Is it addressed to you or your relation? If the mail is not for you or your family, the house is probably not yours. Return the mail to the box unopened.

* **Try your key in the lock.**

Shopping-Mall Safety Tips

* **Never walk unaccompanied through the parking lot.** If you are shopping alone, wait for other shoppers to come into view and walk near them. If you are leaving the mall after dark, request an escort from a mall security guard, especially if you are carrying several packages.

* **Avoid automatic revolving doors.** Thieves can prey on you as you enter the door, using the time it takes for you to complete the circle to make their getaway.

* **Consolidate your purchases.** Combining your acquisitions into one or two large bags will help you keep better track of your possessions.

* **Use the restrooms near the food court or other high-traffic areas.** Avoid bathrooms that are located down service hallways or on quiet floors of department stores.

* **Park in well-lit areas.** Put your car as close to the entrance of the mall as possible. When you are forced to park farther away, make sure the spot will be well-lit, even if it is daylight when you first enter the mall. Park in as well-traveled a location as possible.

* **Stow all packages in the trunk.** Never put packages in the backseat while you return to the mall to do more shopping. Leave all your most expensive purchases for last so you'll never have to leave them unattended.

* **Get your keys out while you're still inside the mall.** Look in the backseat of your car before entering.

* **Remain alert as you unload packages into the car.** Most carjackings occur when the victim is distracted by transferring packages from a cart or securing children into the car. Stay aware of your surroundings.

* **If you suspect that you are being followed, look the presumed assailant in the eyes and yell "Stop."** Then run toward other people, pointing and yelling, or run into the closest store or office. Do not stand your ground.

GETTING RID OF COMMON GARDEN AND HOUSEHOLD PESTS

Pest	Solution
Voles	Weed garden and keep it clear of debris; plant dense ground cover; spread coyote or fox urine around yard; set mouse and rat traps
Groundhogs	Spread epsom salts or ammonia-soaked rags around yard; use flamethrower to destroy underground tunnels
Rabbits	Protect gardens with chicken-wire fence buried at least 1 foot deep; plant foxglove, monkshood, lavender, or catnip
Moles	Plant daffodils or caper spurge; place castor oil–soaked rags in heavily trafficked areas; get hunting cat
Raccoons	Use acoustic repellent system; spread jalapeño or cayenne pepper in heavily trafficked areas
Beavers	Surround tree trunks with heavy-gauge wire fencing
Deer	Spread coyote urine in affected areas; place hot sauce or containers holding chicken eggs in water in heavily trafficked areas
Bees	Place sugar water or soda in open containers in unobtrusive areas to draw bees away
Mosquitoes	Plant rosemary bushes or citronella geraniums; when grilling, toss fresh rosemary leaves on the coals and burn a citronella candle
Mice	Dab peppermint oil on surfaces where the animal has been spotted
Bats	Illuminate area with bright lights and create strong drafts with electric fans; spread bags of mothballs around home to repel the animals
Squirrels (in walls)	Scare them from their lair with loud noise or wait until they leave to forage for food, then cover their entrance in heavy-gauge hardware screen

HOW TO PUT OUT A GRILL FIRE

1 If you can safely reach the knobs, turn off the burners on a gas or propane grill.

If a propane tank itself is involved in the fire, evacuate the vicinity and call emergency services immediately.

2 Smother the fire.

Never spray water onto a grease fire. It will intensify the flames and spread the burning grease to a wider area. Throw salt, baking soda, or sand onto the fire to smother the flames.

3 Close the lid.

Make sure all grill vents are closed to further starve the fire of oxygen.

4 If the fire is still burning after 30 seconds, douse the grill with a fire extinguisher.

Be Aware

Flare-ups are usually caused by excess fat and grease dripping from meat through the grates. To prevent a flare-up from getting out of control, quickly move food to a warming rack with a pair of long-handled tongs. Return each piece to the center of the grill one by one, let the excess fat burn off, and remove it to the warming rack again. When every piece has been treated in this fashion, return all the food to the grill and continue cooking.

How to Extinguish Burning Clothing

1 Stop moving.

Do not run or flail your limbs, as you will fan the fire, drawing in air and causing flames to burn hotter and more quickly. Running will also cause you to inhale smoke and harmful gasses, and you may spread the fire to other parts of your body, onlookers, or nearby objects.

2 Smother the fire.

If you have a fire blanket (or other heavy wool blanket) or bulky covering nearby, wrap it around yourself, patting at the flames.

3 Cover your face with your hands.

4 Drop to the ground.

Lie facedown to protect your head from the flames.

5 Roll over repeatedly.

Continue rolling, as necessary, to extinguish all flames.

6 Treat burn areas with cool water.

Apply liberally. Do not break blisters or disturb charred skin. Wrap burn area loosely in dry, sterile bandages. Do not apply creams or ointments.

7 Call emergency services.

For the best chance of recovering all body function and preventing infection, seek professional medical treatment.

Be Aware

Dense fabrics burn more slowly than light, loosely woven garments. If you are barbecuing, wear heavy, tightly-knit clothing such as denim or canvas. All-natural fibers (wool, cotton) are best since they tend to burn slowly. Synthetic fibers can be extremely hazardous when aflame, as they will quickly melt, adhering to skin and causing severe burns. Never spray fire-retardants on clothing.

How to Extinguish a Lawn Fire

1 Locate fire-suppression tools.
Instruct others nearby to quickly gather a bucket of water, shovel, and rake.

2 Smother the flames.
Apply water liberally or, if none is available, use a shovel to dig soil or sand and cover the fire. A long-handled shovel with a wide blade can be used to swat or tamp out errant flames. Stand well back from blazing grass as you attempt to put out the fire.

3 Clear the area of fuel.
As you dig or tamp, push flammable items, such as leaves or brush, away from the path of the fire.

4 If you are unable to extinguish the fire, use the rake or shovel to clear a path to safety.

5 Call emergency services.

*Douse the flames with any available water
or nonflammable beverages.*

Grilling Safety

* **Grill on level ground at least 10 feet from buildings, trees, or brush.** Do not grill on a balcony, terrace, roof, or any structure that can catch fire.

* **Wear safe clothing.** Avoid untucked shirt tails, loose sleeves, and aprons with long strings. Use flame-retardant grilling mitts to protect hands and arms.

* **Never leave a grill unattended once it's lit.**

Charcoal Grills

* **Never use a charcoal or gas grill in an enclosed area.** Even with a window open or a fan ventilating the area, carbon monoxide produced by burning charcoal or gas can collect indoors and kill you. Carbon monoxide has no odor or color, so you will not be aware of its presence.

* **Do not add starter fluid to an existing fire.** The flame may attach to the liquid as you squirt it on, forming an arc of fire back to the bottle in your hands.

Gas Grills

* **Open the lid before lighting a propane grill.** Gas can accumulate inside the grill and explode upon ignition.

* **Check for gas leaks.** At least once a season and every time you replace the gas tank, mix 2 tablespoons of dishwashing detergent with 2 tablespoons of water, open the gas valve, and brush the solution onto all valve connections, tubing connections, and the welds on the tank. Look for growing bubbles at each location. If you find a leak, shut the valve or remove the gas tank and refrain from using the grill until it has been repaired. Do not light the burners while performing a leak test.

Out and About

Gangs of 20 to 30 marauding monkeys are breaking into homes in suburban developments in parts of Asia and Africa. In Singapore, macaque monkeys will enter housing complexes to raid trash cans, to steal food from picnickers and golfers, and even to invade homes to ransack cupboards. Baboons in South Africa will go so far as to break windows to get inside houses. Once inside, they'll open doors that obstruct their way to the kitchen, steal food from the refrigerator, and defecate on the furniture—even while the human inhabitants are in the house. Residents in the suburbs of Cape Town have hired a team of monitors to stay with the baboons from early morning until dusk, making noise and waving sticks when the baboons attempt to enter their neighborhood. However, some baboons have grown used to the monitors' methods, and on trash day they'll come at night or very early in the morning to evade harassment.

In both Singapore and South Africa, the monkeys' behavior can be blamed on human encroachment into the monkeys' former territory. To help drive the monkeys away from human homes, authorities recommend using special monkey-proof trash bins, leaving all food out of sight, and removing all fruit trees from affected communities.

Out and About

One urban pigeon can produce as much as 25 pounds of highly acidic droppings in a year—in some nesting areas, the layer dung can grow so thick that it can be measured in tons. And the droppings are more than just unsightly. Pigeon dung erodes the stone and metal facades on buildings and monuments, and it acts as a perfect fertilizer for the bacteria and fungi that cause more than 60 communicable human diseases. The most common of these are histoplasmosis, which attacks the lungs, and cryptococcosis, which causes meningitis and encephalitis. Pigeon populations that are specifically fed by humans can reproduce six times per year, much faster than pigeons who scavenge for their own food. Cities such as London and Venice, once known for their pigeons, have taken steps to combat pigeon-related property damage and disease by closing down birdseed vendors, hiring falconers to patrol the city, and introducing large fines for those who actively feed the pigeons.

SELECTED DISEASES SPREAD BY RATS

Disease	Symptoms	Treatment
Hantavirus	Fatigue, fever, muscle aches in thighs, hips, back, and shoulders; after 10 days: coughing and shortness of breath, feeling of band around chest as the lungs fill with fluid	No specific treatment or cure; hospitalization in intensive care unit may help, the earlier the better
Hepatitis E	Jaundice, fatigue, abdominal pain, loss of appetite, nausea, vomiting, dark (tea colored) urine	No specific treatment
Leptospira (Weil's disease)	Early stage: fever, chills, muscular aches and pains, loss of appetite, and nausea when lying down; advanced stage: bruising, anaemia, sore eyes, nose bleeds, jaundice, organ damage	Antibiotics, sometimes intravenously; may be fatal
Listeria (listeriosis)	Early stage: Fever, muscle aches, sometimes nausea or diarrhea; advanced stage: headache, stiff neck, confusion, loss of balance, convulsions	Antibiotics; during pregnancy, can cause miscarriage, premature delivery
Liver Worm	Abdominal pain, diarrhea, weight loss, fatigue, jaundice, fever, cough, asthma, pneumonia	Prescription drugs; may be fatal
Plague	Fever, extreme exhaustion, headache; swollen, hot-to-the touch lymph node; pneumonia with high fever, cough, bloody sputum, and chills	Quarantine, antibiotics; death rate over 50% once pneumonia develops
Rat-Bite Fever	Abrupt onset of chills and fever, vomiting, pain in back and joints, headache, muscle pain, rash on hands and feet, swelling in joints may then become swollen, red, and painful	Antibiotics; can be fatal
Tapeworm	Nausea, weakness, loss of appetite, diarrhea, abdominal pain; often no symptoms	Prescription medication to dissolve worm within intestines

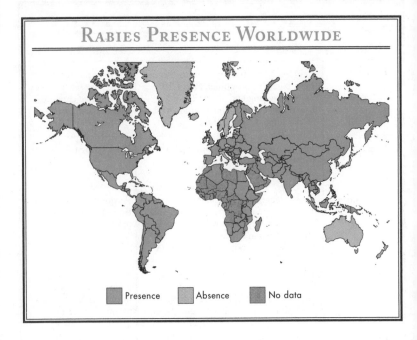

RABIES PRESENCE WORLDWIDE

Presence   Absence   No data

Out and About

Rabies has a 100 percent fatality rate for humans when not treated within 72 hours of exposure. The only recorded case of survival without immediate vaccination occurred in Wisconsin in 2004, when desperate doctors put an infected teenager into a drug-induced coma and administered four antiviral medications. Her recovery was considered miraculous.

COMMON EDIBLE URBAN PLANTS

Species	Characteristics	Habitat	Edible Parts	How to Eat
Amaranth	Cluster of small green flowers at top of plant, simple alternating leaves	Sunny areas, parks, vacant lots	Seeds	Roast and grind into flour
Burdock	Arrow-shaped leaves, pink or purple flowers, large root	Roadsides, sidewalk cracks	Stems and roots	Peel and boil
Dandelion	Leaves with jagged edge, bright yellow flowers, close to ground	Sunny areas	Young leaves; mature leaves; flowers	Young leaves: raw; mature leaves: boil; flowers: fry
Grass	Spiky green stalks	Virtually everywhere	Seeds, blades	Seeds: roast; blades: chew for juice
Oak trees	Green leaves with jagged edges, acorn nuts	Parks, yards	Acorns	Boil, changing water four times before eating
Watercress	Stems float in water, leaves rest on top or above water, clusters of small white and green flowers	Stream beds	Leaves and stems	Raw

SELECTED SOURCES

BOOKS AND INTERVIEWS

Albanov, Valerian. *In the Land of White Death*. New York: Modern Library, 2001.

Alloway, David. *Desert Survival Skills*. University of Texas Press, 2000.

Anderson, Harry. *Exploring the Polar Regions*. Facts on File, 2005.

Bigon, Mario, and Guido Regazzoni. *The Morrow Guide to Knots*. Maria Piotrowska, trans. New York: Quill/William Morrow, 1981.

Blechman, Andrew D. *Pigeons*. New York: Grove Press, 2006.

Boswell, John (ed). *U.S. Armed Forces Survival Guide*. New York: St. Martin's/Griffin, 1980.

Brown, Tom. *Field Guide to City and Suburban Survival*. New York: Berkeley Books, 1984.

Brendan Carr, medical trauma specialist.

David Corr, cement engineer.

DeFoliart, Gene R. *The Human Use of Insects as a Food Resource: A Bibliographic Account in Progress*.

Ellison, Jib. *Basic Essentials: Rafting*. Guilford, Connecticut: Globe Pequot Press, 2000.

Graydon, Don (ed). *Mountaineering*. Seattle: The Mountaineers, 1992.

Hart, John. *Walking Softly in the Wilderness*. San Francisco: Sierra Club Books, 2005.

Christine Huffard, marine biologist and octopus expert.

Jacobson, Cliff. *Expedition Canoeing*. Guilford, Connecticut: Globe Pequot Press, 2001.

Kincaid, Reid. *The Extreme Survival Almanac*. Boulder, Colorado: Paladin Press, 2002.

Lansky, Doug. *Rough Guide to Travel Survival*. New York: Rough Guides, Inc., 2005.

McDougall, Len. *The Outdoors Almanac*. Springfield, New Jersey: Burford Books, 1999.

McManners, Hugh. *The Complete Wilderness Training Book*. New York: DK Publishing, 1998.

McNab, Chris. *How to Survive Anything, Anywhere*. Camden, Maine: International Marine/McGraw-Hill, 2004.

Sacco, Joe. *Safe Area: Gorazde*. Seattle: Fantagraphics Books, 2000.

Sauer, P. and M. Zimmerman. *Complete Idiot's Guide to Surviving Anything*. New York: Alpha Books, 2001.

U. S. Army Survival Manual. New York: Dorset Press, 1991.

Walden, John. *Jungle Travel and Survival*. Guilford, Connecticut: Lyons Press, 2001.

Williams, Jack. *Complete Idiot's Guide to the Arctic and Antarctic*. New York: Alpha Books, 2003.

Willis, Clint (ed). *Epic*. New York: Thunder's Mouth Press, 1997.

———. *Wild*. New York: Thunder's Mouth Press, 1999.

Wiseman, John "Lofty." *The SAS Survival Handbook*. London: HarperCollins, 1986.

WEBSITES

AmericanWhitewater.org

Bermuda-Triangle.org

Bigfoot Field Researchers Organization (www.bfro.net)

Central American Sea Kayak Expedition 2000 (www.caske2000.org)

Crimedoctor.com

Electronic Library of Construction Occupational Safety and Health (www.cdc.gov/eLCOSH)

"Everest," *Nova* (www.pbs.org/wgbh/nova/everest)

EverestHistory.com

ExplorersWeb.com

Food-Insects.com

Frank Slide, Alberta (www3.sympatico.ca/goweezer/canada/frank.htm)

GlobalSecurity.org

Guam official site (ns.gov.gu)
HistoryNet.com
Insects.org
InternationalLiving.com
K2Climb.net
Lawrence of Arabia (www.pbs.org/lawrenceofarabia/revolt/
    navigation.html)
MongaBay.com
MountEverest.net
MSNBC.com
NationMaster.com
PaddleSportsInfo.com
PeakFinder by Dave Birrell
    (www.rmbooks.com/Peakfinder/index.htm)
PrimitiveWays.com
SaharaWind.com
South-Pole.com
"Volcano Above the Clouds," *Nova* (www.pbs.org/wgbh/nova/
    kilimanjaro)
Whales-Online.org

Magazines, Newspapers, Organizations, and Other Sources

ABC News
Alberta Geological Survey, Alberta Energy and Utilities Board
American Lung Association
American Lyme Disease Foundation, Inc.
American Red Cross
Anchorage Daily News
Arctic Studies Center, National Museum of Natural History
Australasian Fire Authorities Council
Australian Broadcast Channel
Backpacker

Blacksmith Institute
Boston Herald
British Broadcasting Corporation
Cable News Network
California Applications Program (CAP) & The California Climate
  Change Center (CCCC), University of California, San Diego
Centers for Disease Control
City Mayors
Construction Safety
Christian Science Monitor
Daniel Boone National Forest, USDA Forest Service
Directors of Health Promotion and Education
Discovery Channel
Economist Intelligence Unit
Encyclopedia Britannica
Federal Emergency Management Agency
Field and Stream
Florida Highway Patrol
Flying Safety
Frank Slide Interpretive Centre
Guardian
Gulf News (United Arab Emirates)
Gulf of Maine Research Institute
Hearth, Patio and Barbecue Association
International Maritime Organization
Manaaki Whenua Landcare Research
Merck, Inc.
Miami Herald
Morgan Quito, Inc.
National Aeronautics and Space Administration
National Broadcasting Corporation
National Climatic Data Center
National Geographic Society
National Health Museum

National Park Service
National Public Radio
National Research Council's Institute for Ocean Technology
 (Canada)
National Safety Council
National Science Foundation
National Weather Service
National Zoo
New Scientist
New York City Transit
New York Road Runners
New York Times
Outdoor Life
Philadelphia City Paper
Public Broadcasting Service
Pulse of the Planet
Scientific American
Smithsonian Institution
Sports Illustrated
Straits Times (Singapore)
Trust for Public Land
United Nations Economic Commission for Europe
United States Department of Energy
USA Today
Wall Street Journal
Washington Post
World Health Organization
World Resources Institute

INDEX

ACKNOWLEDGMENTS

David Borgenicht has come to realize that they don't call it the "great" outdoors for nothing; it's big, complex, and dangerous, but ultimately a thing of incredible beauty—a lot like this book. He'd like to thank his fellow scouts for joining in on this adventure and keeping the troop together with the "buddy system": Melissa Wagner, Jay Schaefer, Steve Mockus, Brianna Smith, Micaela Heekin, Karen Onorato, Trey Popp, Bob O'Mara, and Brenda Brown. Without each of them, this excursion wouldn't have been possible—or, indeed, survivable. And now that it's over, he hopes everyone will actually be able to see the outdoors again.

Trey Popp is grateful for the creativity and resourcefulness of David Borgenicht, Brenda Brown, and especially Melissa Wagner, without whom this book would still be in pencil-and-napkin form. He also thanks his friends and family for supporting—and sometimes even encouraging—his ideas and exploits. Most of all he thanks his wife, Liz, who transforms the routine business of everyday survival into lasting joy.

ABOUT THE AUTHORS

David Borgenicht is a writer and armchair adventurer who grew up in the West, hiking, fishing (using Velveeta cheese as bait), and camping (although he did this mostly out of a Volkswagen Vanagon). He is the coauthor of all the books in the *Worst-Case Scenario* series and the publisher of Quirk Books (www.quirkbooks.com), and he now lives in Philadelphia.

Trey Popp has run out of food in the Borneo rainforest, run out of water in the Australian desert, and run over a goat while bicycling in Bangladesh. He was very sorry each time. He has never run out of good fortune or exceptional friends, both of which have been critical to his survival more times than he'd like to let on. He currently calls Philadelphia home.

Brenda Brown is an illustrator and cartoonist whose work has been published in many books and publications, including the *Worst-Case Scenario* series, *Esquire*, *Reader's Digest*, *USA Weekend*, *21st Century Science & Technology*, the *Saturday Evening Post*, and the *National Enquirer*. Her website is www.webtoon.com.

THE FIRST OF THE WORST

The
WORST-CASE SCENARIO
Survival Handbook

HOW TO:
→ Escape from Quicksand
→ Wrestle an Alligator
→ Break Down a Door
→ Land a Plane ...

By Joshua Piven and David Borgenicht

⚠ 3 million copies
in print

⚠ Translated into
27 languages

⚠ International
best-seller

"An armchair guide for
the anxious."
—*USA Today*

"The book to have when the
killer bees arrive."
—*The New Yorker*

"Nearly 180 pages of immediate
action drills for when everything
goes to hell in a handbasket."
—*Soldier of Fortune*

"This is a really nifty book."
—*Forbes*

A BOOK FOR EVERY DISASTER

⭐ *The Worst-Case Scenario Survival Handbook*

⭐ *The Worst-Case Scenario Survival Handbook:* **Travel**

⭐ *The Worst-Case Scenario Survival Handbook:* **Dating & Sex**

⭐ *The Worst-Case Scenario Survival Handbook:* **Golf**

⭐ *The Worst-Case Scenario Survival Handbook:* **Holidays**

⭐ *The Worst-Case Scenario Survival Handbook:* **Work**

⭐ *The Worst-Case Scenario Survival Handbook:* **College**

⭐ *The Worst-Case Scenario Survival Handbook:* **Weddings**

⭐ *The Worst-Case Scenario Survival Handbook:* **Parenting**

⭐ *The Worst-Case Scenario Book of* **Survival Questions**

⭐ *The Worst-Case Scenario Survival Handbook:* **Extreme Edition**

⭐ *The Worst-Case Scenario Survival Handbook:* **Life**

⭐ *The Worst-Case Scenario Almanac:* **History**